MINUTE GUIDE TO

GETTING INTO COLLEGE

by O'Neal Turner, Ph.D.

alpha
books

A Division of Macmillan Publishing
A Simon & Schuster Macmillan Company
1633 Broadway, New York, NY 10019

International Standard Book Number: 0-02-860616-7

Library of Congress Catalog Card Number: 95-080514

97 96   10 9 8 7 6 5 4 3 2 1

Interpretation of the printing code: the rightmost number of the first series of numbers is the year of the book's printing; the rightmost number of the second series of numbers is the number of the book's printing. For example, a printing code of 96-1 shows that the first printing of the book occurred in 1996.

Printed in the United States of America

Publisher: Theresa Murtha

Managing Editor: Lisa Wolff

Series Editor: Bart Astor

Development Editor: Jennifer Perillo

Cover Designer: Lori Singer

Production Manager: Scott Cook

Production Team Supervisor: Laurie Casey

Designer: Barbara Kordesh

Indexer: Charlotte Clapp

Production Team: Heather Butler, Angela Calvert, Dan Caparo, Tricia Flodder, Joe Millay, Gina Rexrode, Karen Walsh

CONTENTS

INTRODUCTION

Once you've selected colleges that best meet your academic, social, and career focus, you have to figure out a plan to get admitted. This book tells you how to best present yourself to selected colleges through campus interviews, admission applications, grades, standardized test scores, and extracurricular activities.

THE TOP 12 THINGS YOU CAN DO TO HELP YOU GET INTO THE COLLEGE OF YOUR CHOICE

Let's start with a fairly detailed summary of *key* points in this book. A clear understanding of each of these points will lead you in the right direction and will guide you throughout the process. With these 12 items as your guide, you won't be wasting time or taking wrong turns.

1. Take the most challenging courses (Regular, Honors, Accelerated, or Advanced Placement) in which you can get good grades (As and Bs).

2. Learn which colleges request campus interviews and prepare for them by being ready to discuss:

   - your reasons for visiting that particular college

   - your values as a student, member of the community, and person

   - your questions about the college

3. Review each application *before* starting to dig into it.

4. Prepare a resumé detailing your activities and motivations, which you can attach to your college applications.

5. Ask people who know you well (teachers, peers, parents, employers, coaches, etc.) and who can express their views to write letters of recommendation for you.

6. Write several drafts of your essay and share them with others.

7. Make sure you meet all admission and financial aid deadlines.

8. Prepare a letter that you can add to your applications that will:

   • highlight your strengths and address your weaknesses

   • express what you and others consider your special features

   • share your serious interest in that college

9. Update your application with:

   • recent grades

   • additional accomplishments

✗• more recommendations from people who know you well and who can present you in a different light than one already viewed

10. Keep your grades up even *after* you apply.

11. Meet with alumni interviewers from your top-choice colleges.

12. Keep in touch (by telephone or mail) with the people who interviewed you at the colleges or who met you at your high school.

CONVENTIONS USED IN THIS BOOK

Throughout this book, you will find three types of icons to help you quickly find important information:

 Timesaver Tip icons offer ideas that cut corners and avoid confusion.

 Plain English icons appear to define new terms.

! **Panic Button** icons identify potential problem areas and how to solve them.

Acknowledgments

This book is dedicated to my various families:

- my immediate family—Debbie, O'Neal, and Ashley Turner
- my extended family of Turners, Froles, Schaefers, and Vignals
- my family at Culver Academy
- my family of colleagues, both high school counselors and admission professionals

The Author

O'Neal Turner, Ph.D. has been active in the field of education since his graduation from college. At the secondary level, he has been a teacher, director of college counseling, and an independent college counselor. At the collegiate level, he has worked in admission offices at Colby College and Georgetown University. He was Director of Admission at Ohio Wesleyan University and Dean of Admission at Butler University. He is currently the Dean of Enrollment Management and College Advising at The Culver Academies, in Culver, Indiana.

GETTING INFORMATION FROM COLLEGES

In this lesson you will learn how to contact college admission offices and request admission material. You will also learn what material to request.

GETTING STARTED

The process of getting into college starts with requesting material from college admission offices—either by calling or by writing to the admission offices at each college you wish to explore. To do either, you need the addresses and telephone numbers of the colleges you are considering. This information is readily available through handbooks and guides in your local bookstore, high school, or library. Some sources include:

Lovejoy's College Guides (Simon & Schuster)

The College Handbook (The College Board)

Peterson's Guides to Four-Year Colleges (Peterson's)

Profiles of American Colleges (Barron's)

1

GETTING INFORMATION BY PHONE

Now that you have those telephone numbers, you can put them to good use. Note that many colleges provide toll-free 800 numbers that cost you nothing. However, if you use an 800 number, be prepared for the phone to ring a bit longer than usual before being answered.

 **Prepare Yourself.** Before you call a college admission office, consider what you would like to request from the college and recognize that the admission office may want information from you as well.

At a minimum, you should request the following information from each college:

- **Application for admission**—if the current one is not yet available, ask for an old one to look at—they change very little from year to year

- **Paper application**—request either the college's own application or the Common Application

- **Disk application**—several colleges subscribe to services through which you can complete one application on a computer disk and forward it to particular colleges. Also, an increasing number of colleges offer their own application on disk. Simply inquire about the available options.

Common Application. The Common Application is a standard application accepted by nearly 140 colleges. You simply complete the application, copy it, and mail it to however many of the 140 to which you choose to apply.

- **Financial aid brochures**—don't think you will not qualify for financial aid. Request information, explore it, then decide.

- **College catalog**—with a complete list of courses offered

- **Viewbook**—detailed pictorial account of the college

Picture Perfect. The photographs in college viewbooks are always beautiful. Don't get snowed by the presentation *until* you visit the campus.

- **Video**—a visual presentation of the college

- **Campus visit guide**—map, directions, office hours, and lodging accommodations near campus

- **Information about specific academic majors and/or departments**—ask for those areas you are considering. Don't be shy about asking for information about several departments.

- **Extracurricular activities**

- **Campus visitation programs**—descriptions and dates of these one or two long programs

- **Names of any current students or graduates in your geographic area**

It might be wise to use a *Telephone Request Log* like the one illustrated in Figure 1.1 to keep track of what you have asked each college to send you.

TELEPHONE REQUEST LOG

Name of College _____ Date Telephoned _____

Material Requested:

❏ application for admission (sending new or old)

❏ financial aid information

❏ course catalog

❏ viewbook

❏ video

❏ campus visit guide

❏ academic majors and/or departments information _____
areas: _____   _____

❏ extracurricular activities
areas: _____   _____

❏ campus visitation programs

❏ names of any current students or graduates in your geographic
area.   details: _____

Name of the person taking this request _____

Date material will be mailed _____

Figure 1.1 Example form to manage phone information requests.

GETTING INFORMATION BY MAIL

Requesting admission material through the mail is quite easy. You can request the same information using a sample form letter like the one in Figure 1.2.

Date
Name of Director/Dean of Admission
Title
Name of College
Street Address
City, State, Zip

Dear (*Name of Director/Dean of Admission*):

I am currently a student at (name of your high school) and am very interested in learning more about (name of the college). Please forward the following to me:

___ application for admission

___ financial aid information

___ college catalog

___ viewbook

___ video

___ campus visit guide

___ academic or departmental information regarding:

_____   _____

___ extracurricular activities:

_____   _____

___ campus visitation programs

___ names of any current students or graduates in my geographic area

_____

      Thank you in advance for your assistance.

Sincerely,

Signature
Name
Street Address
City, State, Zip
Telephone
Social Security Number

Figure 1.2 Form letter for requesting material from colleges.

After you've requested your college information, your name will be placed on the college mailing list. Most colleges continually send a flow of material to students on this list.

tip **Phone First.** If you are given the option of requesting material either by phone or by mail, use the phone. In case the material does not arrive soon, take the name of the person you speak with so you can ask for that person the next time you call.

SUMMARY

In this lesson you learned where to obtain addresses and telephone numbers of admission offices. You also learned the specific items to ask for when requesting material and the correct format for both telephoning and writing for information.

CHECKING OUT THE COLLEGES

In this lesson you will learn some of the ways to gather information about colleges and how this knowledge can help you get in. These ways include exploring the colleges through the material they send you, contact with others, and visits to the campuses.

To gain admission to colleges that are the best "fit" possible, fully explore those institutions that interest you. Any such exploration should include information both *from* and *about* these colleges. Opinions from others (counselors, current students, graduates, friends, family) are essential; at the same time, one of the best ways to check out a college is by visiting the school. This visit can serve three purposes: One, you can get a first-hand perspective of the school. Two, you help the admission office check out whether you'll be a good match with the college. And three, a visit can help you get in.

USING THE MATERIAL FROM THE COLLEGES

In Lesson 1 you learned the process by which you request material from colleges. Once this information arrives, it's time to

examine it carefully to see whether there's a good match between you and the college. One way to tell if there is such a
match is to ask yourself the following three questions:

1. What initially attracted me to this college?

2. After reading the material from the college, how
   do I *now* feel about specific issues such as:

   * Breadth of the academic programs
   * Campus facilities
   * Location of the college
   * Faculty–student interaction
   * Size of the student body
   * Distance from home
   * Extracurricular activities
   * Options after graduation
   * Cost and availability of financial aid

3. What is truly special about this college that would
   make me want to explore it further?

USING INFORMATION FROM OTHERS

You should now have a clearer sense of what the college has to
offer from the material the college provided. Now would be a
good time to review the opinions of others. One way to explore these views is by reading perspectives of colleges from

current students or reviewers. Typically, surveys are distributed to students attending these colleges, their opinions are compiled, and a reviewer molds a description from the survey results. In recent years, a number of these books have been published, including the following:

- *The Selective Guide to Colleges*, by Edward Fiske

- *The Insider's Guide to the Colleges*, by the Editors of the Yale Daily News

- *The Princeton Review Guide to the 306 Best Colleges in America*

- *The 100 Best Colleges for African American Students*, by Erlene Wilson

Although printed material has its place in assessing colleges, live human beings can be even more helpful. Caution: Don't just talk to your friends. Try to get input from all these sources:

- College advisor/Guidance counselor

- Students currently attending these colleges

- Graduates of the colleges

- Friends who are also exploring colleges

- Family members

- People working in a career that interests you

- Coaches

- Clergy

> **tip**
>
> **Good Sources.** The more these individuals know about both you and the college, the clearer their assessment of the match between the two of you will be.

USING THE CAMPUS VISIT

The best way to determine if a specific college is a good match for you is to visit it. To use a popular analogy, you wouldn't buy a $40,000 car without test driving it, so why would you choose to attend a $50,000–$125,000 college without first visiting?

Equally important, some admission directors believe that a greater percentage of students who visit will enroll. Since colleges are competing for students, these admission directors view the applications of students who have visited in a more favorable light than applications of students who have not visited—even if those students are stronger academically. After all, visiting demonstrates an enthusiasm for the college that means, if accepted, you're more likely to enroll. So, in some instances, these visits to campus can strengthen your chance of admission.

When scheduling a campus visit, you should do the following things:

- Plan ahead—a minimum of two weeks ahead is reasonable
- Budget your time—plan a minimum of four hours on campus

- Schedule by phone—conflicts are more easily handled by phone than mail

- Have a date and time in mind—weekdays are best, but be flexible

- Request a meeting with others, such as financial aid officers, faculty, coaches, and so forth

- Choose a personal interview over a group session if you have the option

- Ask if it's appropriate to bring your resumé and high school transcript to the interview

- Start with your personal interview first, if possible, then tour—it's better to be fresh for the interview

- Get the name of the person scheduling your visit

- Get written confirmation of your appointment from the person scheduling your visit

Many colleges offer prospective students the chance to stay overnight on campus. You will be assigned a current student as your host to take you to classes, social functions, and athletic and/or performing arts events. If you're interested in such an experience, ask the person scheduling your visit about this opportunity.

Package Visits. A growing number of tour organizations offer campus visit packages of 8–12 campus visits per trip. During the campus stay, students have the opportunity to tour the campus and to participate in a group session/interview in the admission office. Two such organizations offering these tours are College Impressions (617-843-8033) and College Visits (800-944-2798).

SUMMARY

In this lesson you learned how to evaluate material from colleges, how to use information from other sources, and how to plan a campus visit.

3

USING THE
CAMPUS VISIT
TO HELP YOU GET
ADMITTED

*In this lesson you will learn the components of the
campus visit. You will also learn how to use this visit to
further your chances of getting into the college of your
choice.*

There are four components of a thorough visit to a campus:
the group session or personal interview, a meeting with the
financial aid office, a tour of the campus, and the campus
"walkaround." While the purpose of these tour components is
information gathering, you can use them to help you get admitted. One of the most important meetings you will have
during your campus visit is the meeting with a representative
from the admission office.

GROUP SESSION OR PERSONAL INTERVIEW

While a few colleges offer you the option of either a group session or a personal interview, most give you no choice. Though different in format, the goal is the same—sharing information about the college. Nevertheless, there are things you can do in either situation to further your chances of getting accepted.

The group session is a presentation of the college to students and their families by a member of the admission office. It typically includes viewing the college video and an extensive question-and-answer period. Aside from the question-and-answer period, there is usually no contact with the admission representative. Generally, the group session is offered at medium-to-larger-sized colleges.

The personal interview is a discussion between you and an admission representative. If done well, it closely resembles an extensive and detailed conversation between two new acquaintances. This is an outstanding way not only for you to learn a great deal about the college, but also for the interviewer to learn about you. In many cases, the interviewer evaluates you by the presentation of your academic record and extracurricular activities, by your personality, and by your preparedness. The personal interview is generally offered by smaller colleges.

tip

Getting Personal. When scheduling a personal interview, ask if the session is primarily informational (designed for you to learn about the college), evaluative (designed for the admission office to evaluate you), or both.

Whether or not the personal interview is used by the college to evaluate you, it is always wise to be prepared for the session. To prepare for the personal interview, you should do the following:

1. Dress neatly and comfortably. Give the impression that this interview is important to you.

2. Bring a resumé and copy of your high school transcript.

3. Review thoroughly the material both *from* and *about* the college.

4. Examine the reasons that have led you to visit the college.

5. Be prepared to discuss in some detail why you have decided to visit the college.

> **!** **Polish Your Skills.** Practice your interviewing skills on colleges that are less important to you so you can be more polished for those colleges in which you have the most interest.

MEETING WITH THE FINANCIAL AID OFFICE

With the cost of higher education growing each year, more families are relying on assistance from financial aid offices at colleges. With this in mind, a visit to the financial aid office can be critical in your college-selection process. While a visit may not have a direct effect on whether you get in, it will certainly demonstrate your sincere interest in the college. And the information you learn may prompt a lively discussion in a personal interview. And, of course, there's always the possibility that what you learn from the financial aid representative will help you get a few more dollars to pay for your education.

Need Blind or Not? Some colleges view applications of students applying for financial aid in a less favorable light than those not applying for aid. Other colleges maintain a "need blind" policy of not considering whether a family is applying for aid when considering applications. *It is a wise idea to ask about, and clearly understand, the policy of each college you are considering.*

Maintain Your Relationship. Keep in close and continuous contact with the financial aid representative. Working with this person throughout the process can save countless hours and may result in additional funds.

Using the Campus Tour to Help You Get In

The tour of the campus is nothing less than a moving sales pitch. From the route taken across campus, to the comments made (or not made) by your guide, from the answers to your questions, to even the clothing of the guide, everything is scripted, packaged, and polished by the admission office. If you realize, expect, and view the tour in this manner, you already have one-half of a great tour, that is, the proper attitude. The other half centers on knowing what to look for, knowing what to ask, and knowing where to revisit during your "walkaround" after the tour.

During your tour you will be shown a great many areas of the campus. Use your observations to make an impression on your personal interviewer or in your follow-up correspondence.

After your tour is complete, consider ending your visit to campus with a "walkaround." Recognize that this is your chance to explore and to confirm or deny what you have learned about from the material, from others, from your group session/interview, and from the tour.

Summary

In this lesson you learned that by visiting colleges you can not only gain first-hand knowledge of the colleges, but you may also increase your chances of gaining admission.

MAKING THE MOST OF THE PERSONAL INTERVIEW

In this lesson you will learn how to make the most of your interview. You will learn the 10 things to do in an interview and how to prepare for the three major questions in any interview. You will also learn how to write an excellent thank-you letter to the interviewer.

THE RIGHT ATTITUDE

Many students are intimidated by interviews, but in reality interviews are nothing more than conversations or exchanges of information and impressions.

When you stop to think about it, both you and the college interviewer have common goals:

- You both want to "sell" something—the interviewer is pushing the college, and you are pushing yourself.

- You both have questions.

19

- You both want answers.

- You both want to make a good impression on the other.

Remember, you have already done your homework on every college you're visiting. *Frankly, at this point you are probably better prepared than 99 percent of all students who interview on college campuses.*

~~1~~0 THINGS TO DO IN AN INTERVIEW

1. Arrive early—15–20 minutes before the scheduled appointment time.

2. Greet the interviewer with a firm handshake— Admission officers meet hundreds of students each year, and most people judge others based on first impressions. Try to find a balance between the Vulcan death-grip and a wet noodle.

3. Introduce those who are with you—After introducing yourself, politely introduce whoever is with you: "(name of interviewer), I would like you to meet my (friend/ parents/ relative)." Not only is this the polite thing to do, but it also puts everyone at ease.

4. Bring materials with you—A resumé (see Figure 4.1) or a copy of your academic transcript. You

might also want to bring a list of questions (see Lesson 6) to the interview. The key is to be prepared.

5. Get comfortable—After entering the interviewer's office, make yourself comfortable.

6. Smile and enjoy the interview—If you prepared as suggested, you'll do fine. This person wants to learn about you. Enjoy being in the spotlight.

7. Speak directly to the interviewer—Make as much eye contact as possible.

8. Open your mouth and talk—Try to use more than one or two words to answer a question or share a thought. Let the interviewer draw you out and see what and how you think and what you want from college and from life. Relax and share.

9. Don't forget to breathe—Remember to stop and breathe when speaking. Think about the points you are trying to make and the questions you are answering. Moments of silence while you gather your thoughts demonstrate confidence and clear-headedness.

10. Be yourself—Talk about your interests outside school, your family, your friends, and your goals for the future. Remember, the interviewer is not looking for anything other than you.

Ashley Joseph O'Neal
1234 Your Street
Big Deal, MO 56789
(123) 567-7890

Academic Record

Culver Academy, Culver, IN (1993–present)
3.45 Grade Point Average (six semesters)
Accelerated Courses—Honors English 10,11 and AP Biology 11
1200 SAT (590 verbal—December 1995) (610 math—May 1996)
28 ACT (June 1995)

Extracurricular Activities

- Culver Academy
  Varsity Baseball—Pitcher—9–11
- Student Council
  —Vice President of Class—12
  —School Treasurer—11
- School Newspaper—*Golden Cougar*
  —Editor of Editorial Page—12
  —Advertisement Manager—11
  —Writer—9–10
- Community
  Aide to Nurse's Aide—Sunnyview Nursing Home—9–12
- Church
  Lector at monthly service—St. Elizabeth Seton—10–12
- Employment
  Counter person—McDonald's (20 hours per week)—10–12

Awards or Honors

- Boy's State Representative—one of three boys from county
  chosen to serve as representative at annual meeting—11
- National Honor Society—11
- All-County Pitcher—selected with record of 9 wins, 1 loss—11
- Debbie Frole Prize for Community Service—12

Figure 4.1 Sample student resumé.

The Big Three Questions

There are only three really *essential* questions asked by an interviewer in any interview:

1. Why are you here?

2. What's your story?

3. What questions can I answer for you?

The questions may not be asked in that order and they may not be that simple. If you are prepared to give detailed and complete answers to these questions, however, you will have an *outstanding* interview. Let's spend a few moments exploring each of these three questions.

Why Are You Here?

Though asked in many different ways, this is usually one of the first questions asked in an interview. The answer may indicate your seriousness about the college, and the thoroughness with which you answer sets the tone for the entire interview. If you appear logical and prepared, you will start to convince the interviewer that you are a good match for the college. Share the specific reasons that have led you to sit in the interviewer's office. Some suggestions include:

1. "I'm looking at colleges that have certain features that are important to me, such as: (insert features such as size, location, setting, etc.)." These specific features will only reinforce the opinion of the interviewer that your reasons are logical.

2. "I've reviewed your material and I'm impressed
    with certain features/programs like: (share those
    features that impressed you from the informa-
    tion)." This answer indicates that you've done
    your homework.

3. "I was referred here by a counselor/friend/family
    member who knows me well and thinks this col-
    lege might be a great match." This answer indi-
    cates that you have explored much more than just
    written material from or about the college.

WHAT'S YOUR STORY?

You may find it very difficult to talk about yourself. You may
be shy, or perhaps you may not know where to begin. So try to
break down your story into three areas:

1. Talk about yourself as a student. And be prepared
    for a follow-up question. Share information
    such as:

    - Grade point average (GPA)

    - Rank in class

    - Honors or accelerated courses

    - Standardized test (SAT or ACT) results

2. Talk about yourself outside the classroom. Share
    information such as:

    - Clubs of which you are a member (both
      school and community)

- Sports in which you participate

- Hobbies

3. Talk about yourself as a person. Share information such as:

  - Goals for the future

  - Career interests (including any jobs held)

  - Family and friends

WHAT QUESTIONS CAN I ANSWER FOR YOU?

This question, and your response, is absolutely critical. Under no circumstances should you say, "None."

This is your chance to obtain specific information or address any concerns. In addition, it is an excellent opportunity to show, not only what you know about the college, but that you have specific questions about this college.

By reviewing material about the college you will focus on questions you really want answered. Therefore, the key to answering this interview question is to read the college's material carefully, create a list of questions, and be prepared to ask them during the interview. Examples of the types of questions you might want to ask include:

1. I've been looking at (name a few colleges and make sure they are similar in size, location, and setting to the one you are visiting) colleges. What features do you feel distinguish your college from them?

2. What specific changes are planned for this college in the next two, five, ten years?

3. I've reviewed your material and think the advising system looks interesting. How likely is it that I will be assigned an academic advisor in my prospective major during my freshman year?

4. Based on my resumé and high school transcript, how competitive an applicant am I for this college?

THE THANK-YOU LETTER

Don't make the mistake some students have made at the end of a long and successful interview—forgetting to say thank you. Not only is expressing appreciation the nice and polite thing to do, it is also the smart thing to do. Most interviewers are also decision makers who select the freshman class. By writing a fairly detailed letter of appreciation, not to mention an occasional follow-up note with highlights of your senior year, you might enhance your chance of gaining admission.

Figure 4.2 shows an example of a well-written letter that could make a positive impression. This is only a sample of the type of letter that could help. Make sure you write your own, using this only as a loose guide.

Date (*preferably within 7–10 days of the meeting*)

Dear (*Name of Interviewer*):

Thank you for taking the time to meet me last week when I visited (*name of college*).

I sincerely enjoyed our interview. As an athlete and potential business major, (*college name*) seems to offer an exceptional balance with (*fill in*):

- extensive internships in the (*geographic area*)—especially with (*certain companies discussed*) so close by

- close student and faculty interaction

- outstanding athletic facilities and a beautiful campus

- strong sense of community based on the (*activities discussed*)

After our conversation, my parents and I took a tour of the campus. We especially appreciated (*tour guide's name here*) extensive knowledge of the courses and requirements of becoming a business major. Her honest responses (which, by the way, matched yours) were especially appreciated.

I also enjoyed my visit to (*name of class*). Professor (*name of professor teaching the class*) discussed some principles of (*subject discussed*) that I am familiar with from my high school class. He was kind enough to spend 15 minutes with me after class sharing his views of the college. Without question, (*name of professor*) made a very positive impression.

Ms. (*name of financial aid counselor*) was also very helpful in discussing the many financial options available to me and my family. My parents were especially thankful to learn more about the financial aid process and merit scholarship opportunities.

If you don't mind, I would like to keep you posted on my academic performance and extracurricular activities throughout my senior year. I will write to you every couple of months to keep you up-to-date.

(*Interviewer's name*), thanks again for a great visit to (*name of college*). It is a wonderful place. I hope to have the opportunity to join your community in the near future.

Sincerely,

(*first and last name*)

Figure 4.2 **Example of interviewer thank-you letter.**

Several things make this a good letter:

> Personalization—This letter reminds the interviewer of a number of things they discussed. Therefore, the interviewer remembers not only the student's name but also the conversation.

> Specific names—The fact that the student mentioned the names of the tour guide, the professor, and the financial aid counselor gives the interviewer an idea of this student's thoroughness.

> Future contact—The fact that the student said that he will be in contact in the future means that the interviewer is likely to look for these letters and enjoy following the progress of the student.

SUMMARY

In this lesson you have learned the purpose and format of the personal interview. You have also learned how to prepare responses to the three major questions asked at an interview, and you were given an example of a thank-you letter to the interviewer.

ANSWERING INTERVIEW QUESTIONS

In this lesson you will learn the four keys to answering questions in an interview. You will also learn the types of questions asked by interviewers, how to analyze them, and how to formulate a response. Finally, you will learn how to avoid "trap" questions.

Admission professionals have their own ways of interviewing; their approaches vary from their overall styles to the specific questions asked. Some ask the same questions of each student. Others do not have set questions but prefer to go with the flow and see where the conversation leads them. Regardless of the approach, there are four things to remember:

1. Listen to the question. Don't answer until you have heard and understood the entire question. If you don't understand the question, ask for clarification.

2. Think about the question. Resist the temptation to blurt out the first thing that comes to mind. A moment of silence for you to gather your thoughts is acceptable.

3. Answer the question once. Don't feel you need to wrap the question in three answer boxes. One thorough, carefully considered response is plenty.

4. Always be prepared to answer "why." Few people have developed the ability to answer the question first and then fully explain their reasoning. Admission interviewers may care more about the *why* than your initial response. Therefore, always be prepared to go deep below the surface questions and answer "why?"

GENERAL TYPES OF QUESTIONS

In Lesson 4 you learned the three major questions in any interview. While the first two questions—"Why are you here?" and "What's your story?"—may seem fairly basic, they are rarely asked in this manner. Rather, these general questions fall into a variety of specific categories, such as:

- Goals
- College
- Strengths and weaknesses
- Academic issues
- Extracurricular interests and abilities
- Personal odds and ends
- Others

INTERVIEW QUESTIONS, LOGIC, AND RESPONSES

Now let's look at some actual college interview questions, determine what they are really asking, and see tips for forming solid responses. Additional questions can be found in Appendix A. For most of these there are no wrong answers, only *your* answers. And there are some responses that are better than others. View these questions and their rephrasing ("In other words") and the possible responses from your perspective.

GOALS

1. **Question:** What goals have you set for yourself that you have already accomplished?

   In other words—In reviewing your accomplishments to date, what have you done that is a result of having a goal and meeting it?

   Response: While it is natural to consider this question in reference only to academics, consider also including other areas of your life.

2. **Question:** What will be the good life for you in 10 or 20 years?

   In other words—How do you see yourself and what's important to you in the future?

   Response: Carefully consider more than just your career. Also consider your family and your role in "other" communities.

3. **Question:** When I say the word "success," what comes to mind?

In other words—How broadly do you view your role in society?

Response: Be careful to view this question in a variety of ways.

4. **Question:** What motivates you to succeed?

   In other words—What drives you to move forward in your life?

   Response: Consider discussing people and situations that have motivated you in the past.

5. **Question:** What are your goals immediately after college?

   In other words—Are you somewhat of a forward thinker?

   Response: Be prepared to share a few interests.

COLLEGE

1. **Question:** What are your reasons for going to college?

   In other words—How deeply have you really thought about this next transition in your life?

   Response: Consider personal as well as career reasons for taking this next step.

2. **Question:** What will you do if you do not gain admission to *any* college?

   In other words—What alternative plans have you made in this unlikely event?

   Response: Rather than trying to discuss myriad other options, consider creating a new list of colleges and trying again.

3. **Question:** If accepted to several colleges, how will you make your final choice?

    In other words—What are the details of your evaluative process?

    Response: Try combining detailed logic (opinions of others, reviewing material) and first-hand experience (visiting or revisiting the colleges) with gut instinct (I really feel this college is the best fit). Try to include something positive about the college.

4. **Question:** What fears do you have about college?

    In other words—How honest are you willing to be with your interviewer?

    Response: Share a few of your fears, such as transition to college, academic concerns, and living away from home.

5. **Question:** How does this college fit your particular needs?

    In other words—Why are you exploring this college?

    Response: Detail what led you to explore the college (size, location, setting, etc.).

STRENGTHS AND WEAKNESSES

1. **Question:** Of what are you most proud?

    In other words—Considering yourself at this time, what do you most like?

    Response: In addition to considering any accomplishments or awards, think about your relationships with others.

2. **Question:** Of what are you least proud?

    In other words—Considering yourself at this time, what do you like least?

    Response: Select a few things about yourself that you would like to change. Avoid discussing something very personal and avoid the standard answers about "working too hard," "driving yourself too much," and so on.

3. **Question:** Now that you have shared with me areas that need improvement, what are you doing about them?

    In other words—Do you have a plan of action?

    Response: Share a plan of action for getting better.

4. **Question:** Which three things do you want me to emphasize about you in my interview assessment?

    In other words—What positive features do you want highlighted about this interview?

    Response: In addition to areas such as academic or extracurricular accomplishments, you may want to emphasize your preparation for the interview and the high degree of seriousness with which you view this college.

5. **Question:** What three adjectives would your best friend use to describe you?

    In other words—Which of your qualities are most noted by someone closest to you?

    Response: Remember, this is your best friend. Select those things that friends would share about each other (loyal, helpful, messy, etc.), rather than adjectives such as nice, handsome, or kind. In other words, be real!

ACADEMIC ISSUES

1. **Question:** What academic areas do you most enjoy in high school? Why do you enjoy them the most?

    In other words—Where do you shine in the classroom and why?

    Response: Select those areas that are readily apparent on the transcript and that you might want to discuss further. In addition, explain why you enjoy this area of study (you're a natural with the material, you enjoy the instructor, etc.).

2. **Question:** What academic areas do you enjoy least? Why do you enjoy them so little?

    In other words—Where do you not shine in the classroom and why?

    Response: Try to share your views on this topic with a balance of offering and explanation, not an excuse.

3. **Question:** Which books have made a lasting impression on you? Describe the impression.

    In other words—What have you read that really meant something to you? Just what exactly did these books say to you?

    Response: Answer the question honestly. Whatever your answer, be prepared to discuss it at length.

4. **Question:** Describe your favorite teacher and explain why you selected this person.

    In other words—Which teacher has been your favorite and why?

    Response: This doesn't necessarily have to be a recent instructor. Again, the *why* is the key.

5. **Question:** Describe an assignment that you especially enjoyed and share why you enjoyed it.

    In other words—What project did you thoroughly enjoy and why?

    Response: Detail the effort and focus on why you enjoyed it.

EXTRACURRICULAR INTERESTS AND ACTIVITIES

1. **Question:** What is the most significant contribution you've made to your school or community?

    In other words—What one thing have you done that has had an impact on your community?

    Response: While not expecting a Nobel Prize activity, select something of which you are most proud and discuss it.

2. **Question:** What extracurricular activities at school have been most important to you and why?

    In other words—What school activities have you really enjoyed?

    Response: Pick a few things that mean the most to you and explain their attraction (teamwork, meeting new people, developing a new interest).

3. **Question:** If you could start high school again, what activities would you participate in that you didn't the first time?

    In other words—What didn't you do in school that you would if you could try again?

    Response: Select something that means something to you.

4. **Question:** What do you do to have fun?

    In other words—How do you enjoy yourself?

    Response: Focus on a few things that might involve others, a few things you enjoy with your family, and a few that you enjoy alone.

5. **Question:** How would either your club sponsor or coach describe you?

    In other words—How do those who interact with you in your extracurricular activities view you?

    Response: This response should be different from that of your best friend. It should take into consideration your relationships with many peers.

PERSONAL ODDS AND ENDS

1. **Question:** What's important to you at this point in your life?

    In other words—What means the most to you now?

    Response: While "personal relationships" might be a great answer, that shouldn't be your only response.

2. **Question:** How are you different now from six months ago?

    In other words—How have you recently changed?

    Response: Carefully select a couple of things that you have noticed and be prepared to discuss the changes. Think about changes that emphasize more maturity, more focus, and so forth.

3. **Question:** What makes you different from everyone else?

In other words—Describe yourself as an individual.

Response: Select a few characteristics that are important to you and explain why. If you're stuck, think for a minute about how your friends might answer this about you.

4. **Question:** Describe two events in the last year that have had special meaning for you.

   In other words—What specifically has happened to you recently that has been especially important?

   Response: Pick a couple of things that truly are important to you, describe them in some detail, and address why they have special meaning.

5. **Question:** How have you spent the last few summers?

   In other words—What have you done, productive or otherwise, over recent summers?

   Response: Share any work, educational efforts (summer school), or travel experiences.

OTHERS

1. **Question:** If our roles were reversed, what would you want to know about me so you could make an intelligent and fair assessment in this interview?

   In other words—What is missing in my questions that may give me a clearer view of you?

   Response: Consider other interviews and share a question posed earlier that you felt gave a special sense of you.

2. **Question:** Specifically how have your parents or other family members encouraged you in your college search?

   In other words—What role have your parents or family played in the college search?

   Response: Share with the interviewer the various types of support and encouragement offered by your family (for example, geographic limitations, cost, etc.).

3. **Question:** Imagine that earlier today you met your college roommate for the first time. Describe in detail your first 20 minutes together.

   In other words—How would you interact with your new college roommate?

   Response: Talk about how you might try to find similarities, preferences, and common ground on which you can grow together.

4. **Question:** Describe some of the pressures you feel as a teenager in society and how you deal with them.

   In other words—What are some of the most difficult issues you deal with as a teenager today?

   Response: Share those things you find most challenging, but manageable, in society (drugs, alcohol, gangs, peer pressure).

5. **Question:** Who is the most important person in your life and why?

   In other words—Who means the most to you and why?

   Response: As always, answer honestly. Be prepared to share why this person is so important to you.

AVOIDING TRAP QUESTIONS

Some questions are obviously more difficult than others. And some interviewers may ask questions that are not so much difficult as they are somewhat sensitive. In many cases, these interviewers are trying to gauge your degree of seriousness about their college. Below are examples of tricky questions interviewers might ask:

1. **Question:** Describe the ideal college.

   Response: You might want to preface your remarks by stating, "Although I don't think any college is ideal or perfect, I'm most interested in colleges that offer (list your criteria)." Remember, because you have selected this college at which to interview, it should have most, if not all, of the criteria you list.

2. **Question:** Which other colleges are you considering?

   Response: Again, because you have selected colleges with similar features, you shouldn't have a difficult time sharing four or five colleges that share many of these features.

3. **Question:** Which college is your top choice?

   Response: Mention the college you are visiting only if it is really your first choice. If you are unsure, you might want to say, "I'm keeping an open mind until I visit each college on my list."

4. **Question:** Is your academic record an accurate assessment of your ability? If not, why not?

   Response: If you feel you could or should have done better in a certain area, then share that view. Don't hesitate to go into detail about your record. However, accept full responsibility for your grades; don't blame others.

5. **Question:** Do you have an opinion about for whom you would vote for president? (or about any similarly controversial issue such as abortion, religion, etc.)

    Response: Most admission interviewers who bring up anything like this are more interested in your reasoning skills and depth of your thinking than your particular beliefs. Therefore, get into this only if you feel comfortable about providing detailed reasons for your views.

SUMMARY

In this lesson you learned the keys to answering questions in an interview. In addition, you learned the various types of questions asked by interviewers, how to rephrase them, and how to formulate a response. Finally, you learned examples of trap questions and how to respond to them.

ASKING
INTERVIEW
QUESTIONS

In this lesson we will turn the tables a bit, and you will learn how to ask interview questions. You will discover the five keys to asking good questions, and you will also learn the two types of questions to ask in an interview.

There is no such thing as a "stupid" question, simply because any question that provides new information is useful. However, there are ill-timed, irrelevant, or badly phrased questions. These types of questions can leave interviewers seriously wondering about your preparation, interest in the college, or ability to do excellent work.

HOW TO ASK GOOD QUESTIONS

Here are five key tips to help you decide what questions will give you the information you need; at the same time, they will leave interviewers believing that they must accept you.

Prepare Questions. Write the questions you have selected on an index card, and make sure they are legible. Don't try to hide the card. Rather, be proud that you are prepared.

1. Don't ask questions for the sake of asking questions. Ask questions you care about. Don't ask a question if you don't want to listen to the answer.

2. Listen carefully to the complete response. If the question is so important to you that you have decided to ask it, why wouldn't you listen to the answer? In addition, be careful not to "cut off" the interviewer in the middle of the answer.

3. Consider the value of asking a follow-up question. After listening carefully to the answer to your question, feel free to ask another related question based on the response. You might want to say, "You just mentioned (whatever), and I have a question about that." This is an excellent sign that you are thinking and paying very close attention.

4. Don't hesitate to ask questions throughout the interview. Recognize that the interview is a conversation; you do not have to hold all your questions until asked.

5. Be courteous about when and how you ask questions. Never interrupt the interviewer. Simply wait until there's an appropriate pause. It is also impolite to ask a question on a totally unrelated topic.

TYPES OF INTERVIEW QUESTIONS

Basically, there are two types of questions to ask in the interview. These are:

1. Questions you ask that supplement the material—"according to your material" questions

2. Questions you ask that are simply of interest to you—"standard" questions

"ACCORDING TO YOUR MATERIAL" QUESTIONS

The first set of questions occur because further clarification of material is necessary. When reviewing information about a specific college, you may have noted a particular point and need clarification. For example, "According to your material," freshmen are assigned academic advisors prior to their arrival on campus. Your question is, "If I choose a major before arriving on campus, am I likely to be assigned an academic advisor who is a professor in that major?"

Notice the first four words, "According to your material . . ." These words indicate that:

- You have carefully reviewed material about this college.

- You are very interested in this college.

- If you put this much energy and preparation into the interview, you are probably a strong candidate for admission.

Carefully review material by and about each college for issues, statements, and policies that cause you to want clarification. Formulate three to five questions by referring to the material before you go into the interview. Carefully listen to the response of the interviewer, and, if appropriate, feel free to ask a follow-up question based on the answer.

"STANDARD" QUESTIONS

The second set of questions are those that are of "standard" interest to you. Unlike the first type of questions that arise from specific material and are different for each college, the second set of questions should be "standards" asked at each college. Select three to five of these questions. Additional questions can be found in Appendix B. Like the thank-you letter in Lesson 4, and the interviewer questions in Lesson 5, these are only general guidelines.

The "standard" questions fall into the following categories:

- Academic issues
- College atmosphere
- Faculty
- Residence life
- Post-college opportunities
- Social life
- Personal perspective

ACADEMIC ISSUES

1. How do you feel college academics will differ from high school academics?

2. What percentage of freshmen (and upperclass-men) enroll in their first-choice classes?

3. What is the level of academic competition (sharing notes, study groups, pooling resources) at this college?

4. Are students involved in the evaluation of faculty? If yes, how are these evaluations used?

5. What percentage of your classes are categorized as lecture classes and what percentage are seminar-style classes?

COLLEGE ATMOSPHERE

1. Describe the sense of school spirit on this campus.

2. Describe the relationship between the college and the local community.

3. How much of a problem is crime on this campus? How do students view the effectiveness of the campus and local police?

4. Describe a typical weekend on campus.

5. How is the atmosphere at this college different from the atmosphere of colleges within a 30-mile radius?

FACULTY

1. How would you describe the level and types of student and faculty interaction (both inside and outside the classroom)?

2. What types of independent work or research opportunities are available for the faculty?

3. What percentage of the faculty are tenured?

 **Tenure.** After a specified number of years, a faculty member may be granted a permanent position at the college. Only under rare circumstances can a tenured faculty member be forced to leave the college.

4. What is the male/female ratio of the faculty, and of what various ethnic groups does it consist?

5. What are some of the common concerns of the faculty?

RESIDENCE LIFE

1. What percentage of students are housed on campus?

2. What are the various types of housing options available to freshmen and to upperclassmen?

3. How are roommates assigned?

4. Please describe your resident advisor system.

5. Please describe the general facilities available in the dorms.

POST-COLLEGE OPPORTUNITIES

1. What percentage of the student body utilizes the various services offered by the Career/Placement Center? When in their college career do students typically use the services?

2. Please share with me any statistics on graduate schools or companies that have accepted students from this college in the last three years.

3. What percentage of the graduates financially support the college within 5, 15, and 30 years of graduation?

4. What types of programs exist here in which gradu-
    ates assist students?

5. What percentage of students who find internships
    are offered employment by those companies after
    graduation?

SOCIAL LIFE

1. What do students do for fun?

2. What are the major social functions of the year?

3. What role do fraternities and sororities play on
    campus?

4. What concerns have you heard students express in
    the past year about social life at this college?

5. What is the best thing about the social life at this
    college?

PERSONAL PERSPECTIVE

1. What excites you about this college?

2. What three things would you change about this
    college?

3. What are the most common concerns you have heard from students in the last two years? What, if anything, is the college doing to address these concerns?

4. Did you attend this college? Why or why not?

5. What is the mission of the college? How is it fulfilling this mission?

SUMMARY

In this lesson you learned how to ask questions of your interviewer, the five keys to asking good interview questions, and the two types of questions to ask in an interview.

MAKING A POSITIVE IMPRESSION IN A GROUP

In this lesson you will learn how to use the group session to both initiate and continue contact with the admission representative. You will learn the 10 things you can do to make an impression that may help you get accepted.

THE GROUP SESSION MEETING

In Lesson 3 you learned that many colleges offer only group sessions rather than personal interviews. Group sessions are not designed for you to make much of an individual impression, but there are things you can do to make a positive impression on the decision makers both during and after the session. In fact, since most students do not explore this avenue, you will have very little competition.

First, let's review the format of the group session. Either before or after the campus tour, students and their families are ushered into a fairly large room. They are greeted by a member of

the admission office staff, and over the next 30 to 60 minutes
are typically:

- shown a video presentation of the college

- given a brief sales pitch

- asked if they have any questions

- thanked for visiting, then dismissed

While it is obvious that you have little opportunity to make
any sort of impression during the first two parts of the session,
you can be positively noticed during the last two.

10 THINGS YOU CAN DO TO MAKE A POSITIVE IMPRESSION IN THE GROUP SESSION

1. Dress in the same manner you would for the per-
    sonal interview—neatly and comfortably.

2. Carefully review material from and about the col-
    lege. Bring both "according to the material" and
    "standard" questions into the presentation. See
    Figure 7.1 for some examples.

> **!**
>
> **Parents Beware.** Many parents view the group
> session as their chance to ask nearly every ques-
> tion under the sun. While your parents' questions
> are welcomed, encourage them to let you ask
> your own questions. Also, note how few students
> ask questions in this session. If you're prepared,
> you will stand out as the star you are.

3. Sit near the front of the room. You are going to ask a few focused questions of the admission representative and you want to be seen clearly.

4. Write down the name and title of the admission representative. You are going to be mailing this individual a very specific letter and you want to send it to the correct person.

5. Ask your questions during the question-and-answer period. While trying not to dominate the session, you want to give the impression that you are *prepared* and *seriously interested* in this college. Ask your questions politely.

6. After the session has concluded, approach the admission representative when the crowd around the person has thinned, introduce yourself, and ask a couple of additional questions. This is a good time to ask if you can present a copy of your high-school transcript and resumé to this person.

7. Within three to five days of the presentation, send a detailed thank-you letter with a copy of your resumé and transcript to the admission representative who gave the group session presentation. Make sure you mark the outside of the envelope "personal and confidential." See the sample letter in Figure 7.2.

8. Telephone the admission representative seven to ten days after mailing the letter. After reaching the person by phone, ask if she or he received your letter. Talk about its contents.

9. Contact the representative through the mail every other month to update your academic and social progress.

10. When sending your original completed application of admission to the admission office, mail the representative a photocopy of your application. Include a note stating:

> *The original application was mailed to the admission office on (date). In that we have worked so closely in recent months, I wanted you to have your own copy. I appreciate anything you can do to give me the opportunity to join your college in the fall.*

"According to your material" questions

- According to your material, all freshmen are guaranteed housing. Could you please share with us the various types of housing available and how the selection process occurs?

- According to your material, over (%) of the students are involved in varsity athletics. What types of academic support do these students receive to help them balance their academics and athletic effort?

- According to your material, this college has a very positive relationship with the surrounding community. Please share with us how this strong relationship was formed and is fostered by the college.

- According to your material, students and faculty have a very positive and interactive relationship. Could you please share some examples of this strong bond both inside and outside the classroom?

"Standard questions"

- What do students do to have fun both on and off campus?

- As a representative of the admission office, what about this college excites you?

- What statistics can you share with us about recent graduate school or job placement?

- Where and when is school spirit most evident?

- Please describe the advising system and how advisors are assigned.

Figure 7.1 Samples of questions related to college material and standard questions about colleges.

Date (*preferably within three to five days of the presentation*)

Dear (*Name of Group Session Presenter*):

On (*date and time*) I attended the group session that you led in the Admission Office at (*name of college*). I sincerely enjoyed the session. As a potential (*subject*) major, (*college name*) seems to offer an exceptional balance with:

- extensive internships in the (*geographic area*)—especially with (*certain companies discussed*)
- close student and faculty interaction
- outstanding athletic facilities and a beautiful campus
- a strong sense of community based on the (*activities of interest*)

After the presentation, my parents and I toured the campus. We especially appreciated the fact that our tour guide, (*name here*), had extensive knowledge of the courses and requirements of becoming a (*subject*) major. Her honest responses to our questions, which, by the way, matched yours, were particularly welcomed.

I also enjoyed my visit to (*name of class*). Professor (*name of professor teaching the class*) discussed some principles of (*subject*) that I am familiar with from my high school class. He was kind enough to spend 15 minutes with me after class sharing his views of the college. Without question, (*name of professor*) made a very positive impression.

Ms. (*name of financial aid counselor*) was also very helpful in discussing the many financial options available to me and my family. My parents were especially thankful to learn more about the financial aid process and merit scholarship opportunities.

Enclosed please find copies of my resumé and transcript. As you can see, I have enjoyed my high school experience, both inside and outside the classroom. I would like to telephone you within the next week or so to learn of your impression of my academic and social activities. I'm interested in learning your impression of the fit between me and (*name of college*).

In addition, I would like to keep you posted on my academic performance and extracurricular activities throughout my senior year. I will write to you every couple of months to keep you up to date.

(*Interviewer's name*), thanks again for a great visit to (*name of college*). It is a wonderful place. I hope to have the opportunity to join your community in the near future.

Sincerely,

(*first and last name*)

Enclosures

(*transcript and resumé*)

Figure 7.2 Sample letter to group presenter.

SUMMARY

In this lesson you learned how to use the group session to initiate and continue contact with the admission representative. You learned the 10 things—seldom used by prospective applicants—you can do to make an impression that may impact positively on your application.

UNDERSTANDING THE COLLEGE ADMISSION APPLICATION

In this lesson you will learn about the college admission application. In addition to learning about the first two parts of the application, you will learn about different types of applications.

The college admission application is the one chance all students have to affect their candidacy. All colleges use the application to obtain basic information such as:

- rank in class

- grade point average

- standardized test scores from SATs and/or ACTs

In addition, some colleges also look at:

- level of challenge in courses

- recommendations from your counselor, teachers, and others

- essay or personal statement

THE ROLES OF THE APPLICATION

The three primary roles of the application are:

1. A voice—The application serves as your voice to the admission office. Through the application you answer the same questions as all applicants, and you can distinguish yourself through the essay or personal statement.

2. A presentation to many—Through the application, your grades, courses, recommendations, and essay are read by many people in the admission office. By reading your application, many people can clearly hear your voice.

3. An equalizer—The application treats everyone as equals. The questions are the same for all applicants. Therefore, all students have the same opportunity to present a clear picture of themselves.

THE PARTS OF THE APPLICATION

While applications vary from college to college, they are all made up of six basic, major parts.

1. Body of the Application

    (a) Personal information—name, address, phone number, Social Security number, place of birth, optional information, parents' occupations and education, and sibling information.

(b) Educational information—name and address of current and past high schools, name and phone number of guidance counselor, and dates of attendance.

(c) Standardized testing information—names of standardized tests, dates taken, and scores earned.

(d) Activities and awards—name and degree of involvement (both hours and years) of activities, jobs held in high school, and awards earned.

2. Short Answer Questions

(a) your interest in the college

(b) the names of other colleges to which you are applying

(c) your academic interests

(d) your favorite books, authors, films, and so forth

(e) any special circumstances the admission office should consider

(f) your career or professional plans

3. Essay or Personal Statement

    (a) typically, this consists of a choice of questions that deal with:

    - significant personal experiences, or

    - opinions about national or local issues, or

    - occasionally, a quote; you are asked to share insights from life in relationship to that quote

    (b) request that you ask, then answer, your own question, or

    (c) request that you write a statement to allow admission office representatives to know you better

4. Secondary School Information

    (a) Form to be completed by your counselor requesting:

    - relationship of counselor to you

    - statement from counselor about your performance inside and outside the classroom

    - view of your readiness to attend college

(b) Official copy of your transcript to be attached listing:

- courses
- grades
- rank in class
- results of standardized tests

5. Teacher Evaluation(s)

(a) Form to be completed by teacher(s) requesting:

- relationship of teacher to you

- statement from teacher(s) about your performance in the class taught by that teacher

- view of your readiness to attend college

6. Other Material

(a) Form to be completed by:

- peer
- parent
- adult who knows you well

(b) Mid-year report/update forms

TYPES OF APPLICATIONS

There are two basic types of college applications:

1. Custom Applications—those from the individual college

2. Common Application—one application representing over 140 colleges

Custom applications are applications that come in all shapes and sizes. These applications are customized to meet the particular admission standards of the college sending them out. Some institutions also have a different or supplemental form for schools within a university (e.g., nursing, education). Read carefully to make sure you have the correct form and all the required components.

The second type of application is known as the Common Application or "Common App." The major advantage to this application is that you complete it only once, photocopy it, and send it to any of the more than 140 colleges that use it to which you wish to apply. This greatly reduces the amount of time you spend on applications and essays. However:

- Do not decide to apply to colleges simply because they are members of the Common Application group. While it might be tempting to use one application to apply to many colleges, it is more important to apply to colleges that match your criteria.

- A number of guidance counselors believe that some of the colleges participating in the Common

Application group prefer students to complete their custom application over the Common Application. Ask your counselor for advice before applying.

APPLICATION PLANS

One of the biggest changes in the college admission process in the last few years is the variety of application plans from which students can select. Be aware that not all colleges offer all options. The options include:

- Early Action
- Early Decision
- Regular Admission
- Rolling Admission
- Open Admission

EARLY ACTION

Under Early Action plans, you can apply by a particular date, usually in the early fall, and receive the admission decision as soon as possible afterward. If admitted, you are not obligated to enroll at the college but may wait until May 1, the National Candidate's Reply Date, to decide.

- Advantages:

    if admitted, you're under less pressure

    you are not required to attend

- Disadvantages:

  you may be denied admission early

  if deferred, your application may be viewed less favorably later

EARLY DECISION

With the Early Decision option, you can apply by a particular date and receive the decision soon afterward. Unlike Early Action, once admitted under Early Decision you are obligated to enroll at the college.

- Advantages:

  if admitted, you're under less pressure

  you have an opportunity to express sincerity to your first-choice college

- Disadvantages:

  you must attend if admitted

  if deferred, your application may be viewed less favorably later

Early Action vs. Early Decision. The difference between Early Action and Early Decision is very important. If admitted through Early Action, you are *not obligated* to attend the college. If admitted through Early Decision, you *are obligated* to attend the college.

REGULAR ADMISSION

This is the traditional option for students. You apply by a particular date and expect to learn of the decision by a standard decision date.

- Advantages:

    you are free to apply without obligation

    stronger students clearly stand out

- Disadvantages:

    you have no opportunity to express first opinion

    you must wait until standard decision date

ROLLING ADMISSION

With Rolling Admission, admission decisions are rendered at various times of the year, depending upon when your application is complete and the caliber of student you are.

- Advantage:

    by gaining admission, you are under less pressure

- Disadvantage:

    if you are not a strong student, you risk not showing better senior-year grades

OPEN ADMISSION

With Open Admission, all students who meet stated minimum requirements are guaranteed admission.

- Advantage:

  admission is guaranteed if you meet certain requirements

- Disadvantage:

  only certain schools—primarily two-year community colleges—offer open admission

Carefully examine the advantages and disadvantages of applying to colleges under these particular plans. When considering particular colleges, pay close attention to the various application options available.

SUMMARY

In this lesson you learned the roles and components of the college admission application, the different types of applications, and the three application plans.

Making Your Application Stand Out

In this lesson you will learn how to complete an outstanding application.

12 Tips for an Outstanding Application

Now that you have a clear understanding of the role, parts, and types of applications, let's carefully examine the steps you can take to make your application stand out from the crowd:

1. Read the entire application first—Before starting to complete it, read the whole application thoroughly. You may think that all applications are alike, but each has its own twists. By reading the application you may come up with an idea about which of your strengths you want to emphasize.

2. Do it yourself—These pieces of paper are both *about* you and *from* you. It is perfectly natural to

71

want others—parents, teachers, siblings, or
friends—to offer their perspectives. However, this
is *your* application. Take total responsibility for the
application by drafting, writing, and mailing the
document yourself.

3. Don't lose track of time—Note the deadlines as
   soon as you receive the application. It might be
   wise to establish a timetable for completing each
   application. Remember, college admission offices
   are likely to question your seriousness if your application is late. Some may feel you are more serious
   and you may gain a small advantage if you submit
   all your material well in advance of any deadline.

4. Follow directions—Directions on an application
   are there for a reason: to ensure that applicants are
   all starting off on an equal footing. Always note
   what needs to be done, by *whom*, and *when*. You
   don't want your application rejected because you
   seem unwilling or unable to follow directions.

Make a Copy. Before completing any application, photocopy the original, and complete the
photocopy. When perfect, transfer the information
from the photocopy to the original.

5. Neatness counts—Neatness is important at all
   times. When completing application questions,
   plan your answers carefully so they fit in the space
   provided. Don't try to scrunch your big thoughts
   into a small space.

6.   Blanks are bad—Don't leave questions blank
     when completing the application. A common area
     where students leave blanks is the biographical-
     information section (name, address, phone num-
     ber, family information, and so on). Also, be sure
     to answer the short-answer questions that colleges
     frequently include on favorite activities or pre-
     ferred academic subjects.

7.   Explain your actions—Always be complete when
     explaining your activities. In addition to listing
     the name of the organization, explain its role on
     campus. Also, it is wise to give more than your
     title when explaining your role in the activity.

8.   Support yourself—Some colleges encourage appli-
     cants to submit material that supports or demon-
     strates their interest in an extracurricular activity or
     academic ability. In response, students submit video
     tapes of their musical, dance, theater, or athletic
     ability. Other students send art work, photographs,
     writing samples, or graded reports. Before mailing
     anything, call the admission office to determine the
     best format and whether this should accompany the
     application.

9.   One additional piece—Many colleges give appli-
     cants the chance to supply an optional statement.
     After reviewing the entire application, ask yourself,
     "What have I not had the opportunity to tell them
     about me?" You could present your thoughts on a
     current event, hobby, or important person in your

life; or you could explain why you feel this college is a good match for you. It's also okay to *not* send an additional statement. If you've said it in your personal statement, you probably should not say it again (more is *not* better).

10. Give it a rest—When you have completed the photocopy of the application, set it aside for a day or two. When you pick it up again, carefully reread it for grammatical, spelling, and punctuation errors. Simply ask yourself, Am I saying what I want to say, the way I want to say it? Now is the time to share your application with trusted friends, colleagues, counselors, or family members. Listen carefully to their suggestions but make your own decisions on what changes, if any, need to be made.

11. Copy the final application—After finalizing any changes, make a photocopy of your application. If for any reason your application is lost, you won't have to start all over.

> **tip**
>
> **Call to Confirm.** About two weeks after you mail your application, telephone any college that does not respond to you with a note stating, "We've received your application." Don't assume they have the application unless they confirm its arrival.

12. Before you drop the application in the mail or hand it to your high school counselor, check to be sure you have done the following things:

- reviewed the application for any signatures that may be required (yours and/or your parents)

- enclosed a check for the application fee (if any)

- attached the proper postage for delivery; remember, if you have added material, it will weigh more and will cost more

ADDITIONAL TIPS FOR EACH SECTION

Following are additional pointers for each of the sections you'll be completing:

PART 1: THE BODY OF THE APPLICATION

1. Be accurate. From now on, you'll be known by your Social Security number. Be certain it is correct.

2. Optional questions are, indeed, optional, with no penalty for not answering.

3. List activities and awards. List them chronologically beginning with those in your senior year and working backward. Group different positions within the same activity before listing the next activity. Absolutely list any honors or awards received, regardless of how trivial they may seem to you.

PART 2: SHORT ANSWER QUESTIONS

1. Show interest in the college. A lot of these questions give insight into your interest in the college, so always be positive and write as if this college was your first choice.

2. Don't try to impress. If asked about a favorite movie or book, don't try to impress the reader with some esoteric book or movie that you don't really care about. Write from the heart.

3. Edit your work. Your writing skills on these short answers should be just as carefully reviewed as on the longer essay. Think carefully before writing and make sure it's edited by a parent, counselor, and/or teacher.

4. Don't make excuses. Don't make up any special conditions, and definitely do not make any excuses for poor performances. If there really are extenuating circumstances, however, this is a great opportunity to explain any shortcomings on your record.

5. You don't have to know what you want to do when you graduate. There's nothing wrong with not knowing what you want to do for the rest of your life. But be sure to at least indicate some interests if asked.

PART 3: ESSAY OR PERSONAL STATEMENT

1. Remember that there are no right or wrong answers. The committee will be assessing your writing skills, maturity, and commitment. So if you have a choice, write on something you care about.

2. Be yourself. Be genuine, sincere, and honest in whatever you write. And don't try to be clever or use big words just to impress.

3. Answer the question. Each essay question is a chance to share your views on the subject of the question. Answer it. Don't use the essay as a chance to squeeze in everything you think about everything else.

4. Edit, edit, edit. Take out extraneous words or incoherent thoughts. Don't ramble and don't feel you must repeat yourself. Write a draft, then rewrite, rewrite, rewrite.

5. Show your work around. Your essay is an important piece of your application. Have others review it, and not just for grammar and spelling. Have trusted teachers, counselors, and relatives give you critical feedback.

6. Write the way you speak. Write in a natural language that is comfortable for you. Vary your sentence length, using both simple and compound sentences (keeping them below 20 words). Avoid

using too many adjectives. You're not writing the
Great American Novel.

In Appendix D, you will find a sample of a completed application. This application represents a composite of those used by
various private and public colleges. The candidate for admission is fictional. Use this material as a guide only.

SUMMARY

In this lesson you learned how to make your application
stand out from the crowd.

WRITING THE APPLICATION ESSAY

In this lesson you will learn guidelines for writing an excellent application essay, you'll explore a valuable tool that helps you create your statement, and you'll view a wide variety of essay topics and response guidelines.

Whatever the application may call it (the essay, personal statement, self-descriptive paragraph) the writing of this piece is the part of the application many students fear the most. This fear is understandable when you consider that many people view writing as a chore and feel that writing about themselves is a cruel form of torture.

It's important to view the essay as a chance to talk, on paper, about the subject of your choice. Unlike other parts of the application where you're given questions you *must* answer, most applications offer you a choice of essays. This should be viewed as an *opportunity* for you to select the topic that most interests you. The essay should be viewed as a window through which the admission professionals can see who you are and why you might make a very welcome addition to their college community.

GUIDELINES TO CREATING A SUPER ESSAY

- Go back to basics—Think about your life to date. Spend a few moments considering your goals, values, education, family, and future. Try to capture a sense of what's important to you. Bring that sense to the essay.

- Go with your gut—Carefully consider the essay options. Select the one that feels right to you. Certain questions may just jump out at you. If you have only one question available, it is probably very broad and will let you express yourself in a wide variety of areas.

> **!** **Choosing a Topic.** When choosing your essay topic, pick the topic that most interests you. Don't feel you must choose the topic most students avoid. You receive no "extra points" when selecting a less popular or more difficult topic.

- Be yourself—Be genuine, sincere, and honest in whatever you write. There are no trick questions in essays. Don't feel you must try to outsmart the question. When you reread your answer, make sure the response is truly yours.

- Follow directions—Remember, you will be compared to other applicants who are answering the same question. If you follow directions when others do not, you will emerge in a more positive light. Therefore, follow word and space limitations.

- Write naturally—It is always a good idea to write in a language that is natural for you. Simple sentences that capture your meaning are very effective. Do not go running to the dictionary and thesaurus, thinking you will impress the admission officer with big words.

- Answer the question—Remember that the essay is a window through which the admission officer can more clearly see you. Don't drape the essay window by failing to answer the essay question. Don't try to be cute, bizarre, or funny; just answer the question.

> **!**
> **Strong Beginning and Finish.** The introduction and conclusion are crucial. Begin with an interesting quote or point, and end with a strong conclusion.

- Have fun with the essay—While it is important to remember the value of answering the question, it is also important to enjoy the process. There is nothing wrong with sharing a glimpse of yourself while answering the question. The best way to determine if you have found this balance is to ask yourself, "When reading this essay, will the admission officer have a clearer sense of me?" If the answer is yes, then go for it!

- Give yourself plenty of time—Create a schedule that permits you to be creative, honest, and thorough, without being rushed. Don't procrastinate until the last minute. In most cases, last-minute work tends to read like it was thrown together quickly. Give yourself time to present who you are.

- Write and rewrite—Many drafts are necessary as you craft an essay. Write a draft that says what you want it to say, then put it away for a day or so. When you come back to it later you will note areas that need work. Several drafts may be necessary until you have a piece that satisfies you.

Read It Aloud. When finalizing your essay, read it slowly and out loud to yourself. By doing so, you'll spot subtle mistakes (like sloppy grammar, disjointed sentences, etc.). And you'll also check the flow from idea to idea and whether your personality comes through.

- Neatness counts—Write, type, or print the essay on anything other than the final essay form. If these pieces of paper are representing you, why would you want to submit something that looks sloppy? Put the final form in a safe place, then do battle with your essay.

- Grammar and punctuation count, too—What you have to say is critical. How you express yourself on paper is also very important. Nothing distracts more from a logical, fun, coherent essay than grammar and punctuation errors. Spend some extra time rereading the essay and running it through a spell-checking process.

- Share the essay—When you're fairly satisfied with the essay, it's time to share it with those people you respect who will give you honest feedback. Remember that simply because you request their viewpoint does not mean that you must satisfy them. Listen to their views, then decide for yourself. After all, who is better to represent you on paper than you?

THE TRIS TOOL

Here is an essay tip that has served students well for many years. It is an easy-to-remember tool that will enable you to focus on what you're saying instead of worrying about the structure of your answer.

Simply remember the acronym TRIS:

T stands for Topic (what you are going to talk about). The topic can be as simple as restating the question. For example: "I have mixed feelings about the question of human rights in the United States today." There you have it: instant introduction of the topic.

R is for Restriction. Often essay questions cover a great deal of ground in only 500 words. Therefore, you must restrict your answer to a particular part of the question, for example: "I feel most strongly about the treatment of minorities and the homeless, and the rights of gays."

I stands for Illustration. Simply put, you state what you have to say about the restricted topic, then illustrate your point with an example, a fact, or whatever is appropriate. Given space or word restrictions, you can include as many illustrations as needed to make your point.

S is for Summary. After you make your point, summarize it by relating it to the point of your essay.

ESSAY TOPICS

Here are several application essay topics. Similar to the types of questions asked of you by the interviewer, as discussed in Lesson 5, you will find "In Other Words" and "Response" areas. Let's start with the response given by Ashley O'Neal in Appendix D.

1. **Question**: If you could have lunch with any one person (living, dead, or fictional), who would it be and what would you discuss?

   In other words—With what person would you like to have a fairly detailed conversation?

   Response: There is no correct or incorrect answer. There is only the answer and the all-important *why*. Ashley answers the question well by focusing on his connection with Robert Kennedy; that is, both feel overshadowed by older siblings and both are interested in politics. Most people reading this essay are left with a sense that it is believable and the conversation would be informative.

2. **Question:** What single accomplishment has given you the most satisfaction and why?

    In other words—What have you done that makes you the most proud?

    Response: Take this question seriously, but provide an answer that gives the reader a sense of who you are as a person in addition to an achiever.

3. **Question:** If you were to describe yourself by a quotation, which quotation would you select?

    In other words—Do you have a phrase or motto by which you live?

    Response: Don't try to create something here if it doesn't apply to you. It may be tempting to find a quotation and write on it; if you have to find a quotation, however, then it may not really mean that much to you.

4. **Question:** What have you read that has had special meaning for you?

    In other words—What book have you truly enjoyed?

    Response: The actual book is really of secondary importance. The real key to this answer is presenting clear, logical, and detailed reasons as to why this book is important to you.

5. **Question:** Discuss an issue of national, local, or personal concern and its importance to you.

    In other words—What issue have you been following closely that you would like to comment upon?

    Response: Many of the students who choose this question do so because they think it will impress the admission office staff, but a less-than-inspired essay impresses no one. Select this question only if an issue means a great deal to you.

6. **Question:** How would you change the education you have received to date?

   In other words—What would you change about your schooling?

   Response: Rather than focusing upon a specific teacher or class, try considering:

   - specific subjects you might have explored in greater detail

   - specific classes you would have enjoyed taking

   - specific requirements for courses or subjects

   - the value of year-round school

> **!** **Don't Second Guess.** Avoid "second guessing" the question. After giving a question some serious consideration, answer it. Remember, there are no "right" or "wrong" answers—instead, there is your serious, considered, and well-thought-out answer.

---

7. **Question:** Describe a humorous experience and explain how you dealt with it.

   In other words—Share something funny and your reaction to it.

   Response: Humor is a very personal thing. It is always difficult to find something that most of us find truly funny. There are three keys to this answer. One, take time to "set up" the incident thoroughly. In other words, draw a verbal picture of the situation so that the readers can see themselves there. Two, describe the humorous occurrence. Three, wrap up the essay by stating your reaction or what you learned from the experience.

8. **Question:** If you could spend a day as you would like, what would you do?

    In other words—What would you do if you had 24 hours and no limits?

    Response: There are lots of ways to answer this question. Some students think it would be most impressive to admission officers if they read, study, or do works of charity. Other students take the opposite approach by saying they would sleep. One memorable response indicated an hour-by-hour list of activities that most of us might enjoy (painting, reading, rock climbing, sunning at the beach, etc.).

9. **Question:** Create and answer a question we did not ask you.

    In other words—What did we not ask you that is important for us to know?

    Response: Some students take the easy way out by finding an essay question from another application and inserting both the question and answer here. That may be fine if you feel you have something to share that is best addressed by that essay. However, it is a better idea to review the application and find something you consider important that the college doesn't know. Create an essay question that solicits a detailed response from you, and then go for it!

10. **Question:** Tell us those things about yourself that will help us know you better.

    In other words—What do you think is especially important for us to know about you?

Response: While this may seem like an easy question to answer, make sure you take it seriously. Your response is an excellent opportunity to highlight those features of you that you want to make sure are noted by the admission office (hard working, loyal, honest, serious about the college).

SUMMARY

In this lesson you learned some guidelines to writing an excellent application essay, explored a valuable tool that helps you create your statement, and viewed a variety of essay topic and response guidelines.

EXTRA
APPLICATION
MATERIAL

*In this lesson you will learn about additional material
you may want to submit with your application. This
material includes letters from others, writing samples,
material supporting special talents, creative items, and a
letter highlighting your interests and abilities.*

Some applicants, and especially some parents, believe that
there are ways they can influence the admission process above
and beyond sending a completed application. Somehow, they
have picked up the idea that additional letters, or something
unusual mailed to the admission office, will impact the decision in a positive direction.

In this lesson we will discuss various types of letters and other
items that have supplemented college admission applications.
You do not have to select any of these additional items; if you
feel one or several might present a more complete picture of
you and your "match" with the college, however, then you
might want to consider adding them to your application. Be
certain to select carefully, though. There's a saying that has
become a sort of rule of thumb among many admission professionals: "The thicker the application file [more extra stuff], the
thicker [dumber] the student."

LETTERS FROM OTHERS

The primary reason to seek additional letters is to provide the most complete view of you as possible. Remember, you wear many hats throughout the week: student, athlete, employee, friend to numerous adults, and so forth. Many of the people you deal with can provide a very clear picture of you that is different from other recommendations. These letters are especially helpful if they contain three elements:

- the writer has an in-depth relationship with and personal knowledge of you

- the letters are honestly written, emphasizing the positive but not ignoring your weaknesses

- the letters are full of examples and anecdotes, not just adjectives

ADDITIONAL LETTER FROM THE HIGH SCHOOL

In addition to requesting recommendations from high school teachers and your guidance counselor, other members of the high school community might have something valuable to share on your behalf. You may want to ask for a letter from the sponsor of a club or organization in which you have made an impact, teachers in subjects other than those requested by the application, coaches you know well, and other school personnel.

EMPLOYER LETTER

A letter from an employer can demonstrate a student's ability to apply his or her learning to real-world situations. In addition, at a job a student might be working with people with whom he or she might not come into contact every day at school. A letter focusing upon the way a student deals with others from diverse backgrounds would be viewed as valuable at any college.

CHURCH OR SYNAGOGUE LEADER LETTER

A letter of recommendation from a religious leader in your community would be valuable if you have been actively involved in a youth group, taught younger members of the community, coordinated social- or religious-related charity efforts, or been an active member at the worship service.

COMMUNITY SERVICE LEADER LETTER

Many students are involved in a variety of efforts to reach out to underprivileged members of their communities. Whether through soup kitchens, food drives, tutoring, or fund-raising activities, many students have helped in their communities. A letter detailing your contributions from an organization leader would add a different perspective to your application.

FAMILY FRIEND LETTER

On occasion, letters from family friends are appropriate. These letters tend to be most helpful in two situations. The first is when, for whatever reason, the family friend is like a parent to the student. In some cases this bond may exist because such a relationship does not (or cannot) exist at home. The second situation is when a son or daughter of the family friend is attending or has recently graduated from the college to which the student is applying. Few people know a college as well as the parents of a student attending or recently graduated from the college.

GRADUATE OF THE COLLEGE LETTER

These letters are helpful only if the graduate is closely involved with, and well-versed about, the college and knows you (not just your parents) fairly well. A letter that can match a graduate's view of the fit between you and the college is very valuable.

> **!** **Graduate Letters.** Make sure you understand any conditions of such a letter. Many graduates will write such a letter only if you plan on attending.

FAMOUS PERSON LETTER

Some parents of applicants spend a great deal of time and effort trying to find someone famous to write a letter of recommendation on behalf of their son or daughter. Unless this famous person knows both you *and* the college, these letters are viewed as very shallow, and they have no positive impact on the application.

WRITING SAMPLE

Many colleges ask that you submit a graded paper with your application. You may want to consider submitting such a paper whether or not it was requested by the college. This paper should have certain characteristics:

- It should be something of which you are especially proud

- It should be something that has been graded (not necessarily an A)

- It should be something with comments from the teacher

MATERIAL SUPPORTING SPECIAL TALENTS

This is an excellent time to include any material you might deem important to support special talents or abilities. If you are an athlete, a performing artist, or a fine artist, you should have already been in contact with that particular department at the college and learned what and how to share your talent in the most appropriate way.

If you have not yet done so, or if you possess talents or abilities that are a bit out of the ordinary, now is the time to share examples through:

- video tapes of your performances

- audio cassettes

- slides of your artwork or collections

If it is important to you, colleges should know about it. After all, how can you present the most complete picture of you if you withhold something important? Unlike the "creative items" mentioned below, these presentations of your special abilities truly represent you.

CREATIVE ITEMS

Quite a few students have stepped beyond the boundaries of submitting their application plus a few letters of recommendation. They have sought attention by submitting wildly different creative materials directly to admission offices. The reaction of admission offices is quite mixed. When these items first started arriving, they were viewed as unique. Recently, many offices view these efforts as little more than an annoying gimmick.

Maybe the dividing line is based on creativity and (most important) what it says about the applicant. If it adds perspective to your candidacy, then it might be interesting. If it looks like a desperate attempt to shore up a mediocre application, then its impact may be minimal at best.

Some creative items that have been sent to admission offices, which you probably should avoid, include:

- the college seal molded in homemade chocolate

- a poem on tree bark

- a photograph of the applicant painting his room the colors of the college

- a medicine bottle with the prescription reading: Applicant needs four years at (name of the college)

- a shoe with a note: "Now that I have one foot in the door . . ."

- a cake in the shape of the school mascot

- daily postcards with new information about the applicant

PERSONAL LETTER

In reviewing your completed application, you might want to consider the idea of drawing particular attention to certain parts that either exhibit strength or need further explanation.

Let's face it, no one is perfect. Things happen that need explanation. If the application does not offer you the opportunity to explain your situation, then you need to find a way to communicate these issues to the admission office.

When you look at your academic record, extracurricular activities, or family circumstances, and you feel you have something to share by way of explanation, not an excuse, then feel free to write a letter and attach it to the front of your application.

Remember to make the letter specific to your particular situation. A sample letter to attach to your application might look something like this:

Date

Dear Admission Committee:

I am writing to you today to share some aspects of myself that I feel you and others at the college might find helpful when evaluating my application to Wonderful University.

As you can clearly see from my academic record, I got off to a difficult start in high school. At the time I entered high school, I simply was not motivated to work hard and earn good grades. I do not share this with you as an excuse but rather as an explanation for my poor grades.

In my sophomore year, I decided to focus my attention on my grades. By the end of my junior year, I was named a member of the National Honor Society. My standardized test scores of 1200 on the SAT and 28 on the ACT also reflect my academic ability.

I have been active in many roles outside the classroom. From student government, to journalism, to baseball, I have tried to contribute to my high school. Outside of school I have been active in my church and community service efforts. Holding down a 20-hour-per-week job has also been a challenge during the last two years. I especially enjoy this effort because it serves as a wonderful outlet from school. When I am working at McDonald's, I focus all my energies in that effort.

I would also like to share my serious interest in Wonderful University. I met with Cheryl Adams during my visit to Wonderful last fall. Since that time, we have spoken on the telephone in an effort to update each other. She has been a major reason why I am so excited about Wonderful University.

As I said at the outset of this letter, I simply wanted to share some aspects of myself with you. I hope you give me the chance to join your community next fall.

Sincerely,

Ashley O'Neal
1234 Your Street
Big Deal, MO 56789
(123) 456-7890

Figure 11.1 **Sample personal letter.**

SUMMARY

In this lesson you learned about additional material you may want to submit with your application. These additions include letters from others, writing samples, material supporting special talents, creative items, and a letter highlighting your interests and abilities.

THE LAST FOUR STEPS

In this lesson you will learn the last four steps of the admission process: (1) the last check before mailing your application; (2) the seven things you can do while waiting that might increase your chances of admission; (3) the ways that colleges respond to applications; and (4) choosing your college.

MAILING YOUR APPLICATION

The "until" time has come to mail your college application. Don't be either too anxious or excited about this *until it leaves your hands*. Before putting it in the mail (or giving it to your guidance counselor), there are a few things to double- and triple-check:

- Have the people you asked to write on your behalf mailed their recommendations to the colleges? A brief reminder might be a good idea.

- Have you included the application fee (usually a check) with the application?

- Did you make a copy of the completed application? The United States Postal Service is good but not 100 percent perfect.

- If you have been in close contact with your interviewer since your first meeting, are you mailing this person a copy of your application to keep him or her up to date?

- Have you included the correct amount of postage? If you have included additional material, one regular stamp may not get it there. You might want to consider Priority Mail, overnight, or guaranteed two-day delivery.

- Are you mailing the application well before the deadline? Hopefully, yes! If you are trying to beat the deadline, then consider mailing it so it arrives by next-day delivery.

- Review your application one more time to make sure you, and in many cases your parents, have signed it.

- Finally, after you have mailed it, don't forget it. As you will learn in a moment, there are things you can do to help increase your chances of admission after mailing the application.

ACTIVE WAITING

You have mailed your application to various colleges. You heave a big sigh and relax, right? Wrong, wrong, wrong—there remain several things you can do and should be doing to increase your chances of admission.

SEVEN WAYS TO INCREASE YOUR ADMISSION CHANCES AFTER MAILING THE APPLICATIONS

1. Contact the admission office at each college and ask if there are graduates of the college living in your area who might serve as alumni interviewers. If the answer is yes, call them and arrange to meet. While it is always difficult to know the degree of impact these individuals have in the admission process, if they are utilized as alumni interviewers they must play some role.

2. Talk with friends who are home from college for spring break. If any of them attend a college that is a top choice of yours, *and* they know you fairly well, ask them to write a letter of recommendation on your behalf. This letter should emphasize the match between you (their friend) and the school (their college).

3. Don't forget your grades. After their applications are submitted, many students let their grades drop. On most occasions, this is not a conscious decision, but rather they simply believe that all colleges will judge them only on what they submit with the application. Wrong. Many colleges telephone high school counselors and ask for a grade update before making the final decision. If your grades continue to reflect strong effort, you may have helped yourself.

4. Continue to be involved in extracurricular activities. One can't help but wonder why a very

involved person suddenly drops all activities after applying to college. If these activities are a major part of your life before you apply, why would you not continue them after you apply?

5. Consider attending any presentation in your area by the colleges. Many colleges "take their show on the road" from September through April. Representatives from the admission office host gatherings around the country. This is an excellent time to discover if the colleges to which you have applied are hosting a function in your area. If so, plan on attending. Be sure to make contact with any admission personnel and let them know you are there. A follow-up "glad to have seen you at the local presentation" letter would be a great way to express continued interest.

6. Call interviewers after sending the application. If you have been in fairly close contact with your interviewers/group presentation hosts, it might be a good idea to give them a brief call. If you sent a copy of your application to them after the original one was mailed, you can now call them to make sure they have received it.

7. Update the college if something has occurred in your life after you have applied. While some colleges provide a form for you to update them (see below), many colleges do not.

Ashley O'Neal might have responded in the following manner on an update form:

Optional Update to Wonderful University

Applicant's Name: *O'Neal*   *Ashley*   *Joseph*

                            Last   First   Middle

School Name and Address:

Culver Academy   1300 Academy Rd.   Culver   IN   46511

School Name   Address   City   State   Zip

Please share with us any updated information that might assist in evaluating your application. Thank you for your assistance.

Is there any additional information we should know about your interest in Wonderful University?

> *Since applying to Wonderful University two weeks ago, I have decided that it is one of my top two choices for college. I can assure you that, if admitted, I will give Wonderful very serious consideration. I am excited about the possibility of joining your community next fall.*

Is there anything that you would like to share regarding your extracurricular activities?

> *Since applying to Wonderful, the manager of McDonald's, John Babcock, has promoted me to Assistant Manager. This added responsibility includes complete closing responsibilities on both Saturday and Sunday nights.*

Have you earned any awards or honors since submitting your application to Wonderful University?

> *Since applying to Wonderful, I have earned three more victories as a pitcher on the baseball team. These wins have raised my season record to 6 wins, 1 loss. Because of these recent victories, I was named <u>Pitcher of the Month for the Northern Conference</u>. I have already informed the Wonderful University baseball coach, Joe Pillar, of this recent award. He seems very interested in having me as a member of the team.*

Signature of Applicant: _____   Date: _____

Figure 12.1 **Sample update letter.**

RESPONSES TO THE APPLICATION

You may soon begin looking at your mail carrier as either the grim reaper (if colleges do not offer you admission) or heaven's angel (if colleges welcome you to their community). Regardless of what the letters say, sooner or later they will arrive, and you will need to know how to deal with them.

OFFERS OF ADMISSION

The best possible outcome to the entire process is to gain admission to at least one college on your list. The goal of the process is for you to have options that excite you. When, not if, this happens—rejoice. You have reached an important goal in your life. It feels great when people want you to join their community!

> **!** **Official Notice.** Many well-intentioned people (graduates, college coaches, faculty members, even your high school guidance counselor) may contact you and tell you of your admission to a particular college. While you should not doubt them, no offer of admission is official until you receive a letter of admission from either the Dean or Director of Admission.

When receiving the admission offer, you need to do two things. First, read the letter to see if there are any conditions of your admission. Some colleges offer admission to students only "if no final semester mark is below a B grade" or "if the student agrees to enroll and pass two summer courses with a

C grade or better." If conditions are part of your letter, make sure you understand and agree to them before accepting the offer of admission.

The second thing is to note the date and manner in which you are expected to respond to the college. Whether you are accepting or not accepting the admission offer, notify each college, in writing, by the requested date, usually May 1. This is especially true if you are accepting the offer. Imagine your frustration if you somehow forget to notify a college (or submit a deposit reserving your space) by the designated date. The result may be that your place in the class is no longer available.

DENIAL NEWS

It is never easy to learn that you were not successful in joining a group of people you really wanted to join. One bit of consolation is, You're not alone. There are many people who were not admitted to their first-choice college. Two things may help you deal with this a bit better:

1. Recognize that you are not a failure—In most cases, the fact that you were denied admission has more to do with the large volume of applicants and less to do with whether or not you were qualified for admission. Simply put, for that particular year, you may not have been as qualified as others for admission. With limited space available, the college selected others instead of you. While that may not make you feel great, it should help you to understand that you shouldn't take the decision personally.

2. Realize that you will have other options—If you carefully read Joseph Allen's book, the *10 Minute Guide to Choosing the Right College*, then you know there isn't one perfect college for you and you probably applied to several good colleges. Instead of focusing on a college that didn't have the good sense to welcome you into their community, redirect your energies to those colleges who have opened their arms to you. Feel good about the colleges that *did* want you.

If your favorite school did not offer you admission, and you would attend if admitted, then you might want to consider appealing the decision. Components of a solid appeal are:

- a well-written letter stating your specific reasons for wanting to attend

- additional grades or information to strongly support your candidacy

- an offer to go to the campus and interview

> **!** **Appeals.** When deciding whether to appeal an admission decision, parents should stay out of the process. The student should be making the call, writing the letters, arranging the interview—not the parents. After all, it was you, the student, who received the letter denying you admission. If you truly want to gain admission, then take charge of the appeal.

If, after all these efforts, no remains no, then direct your attention to a college that has welcomed you to its community.

THE WAIT LIST

Each year, many colleges place a lot of students on a "wait list." Basically these colleges are asking you, "If we have room later, would you like to be considered again?" If the college asking is one of your top choices, you may want to say, "Yes, indeed!" If the college is not a top choice, this is a good time to send in a "Thanks, but no thanks" response.

The secret to moving from the wait list to admission is persistence. If this college is your top choice, you may want to do the following four things:

1. Place a deposit at another college to reserve your place in case you don't get off the wait list.

2. Respond to the wait-list offer with a detailed letter expressing your interest and restating your fit with the college. You may also want to include additional improved grades, recommendations, another essay, or additional honors or awards.

3. After you send the letter, call to make sure the letter arrived. Ask to speak with the admission representative you know best and ask her or him how you can further your chances of gaining admission. You may want to ask about the size of the list, where you fall on it, when they may make offers, and the recent history of such a wait list at that particular college.

4. Ask your guidance counselor to telephone the representative you have been talking to and re-emphasize your seriousness about that particular college.

After all this effort, it is very possible that the college won't accept any—or very few—students from the waiting list. Knowing that you put forth your best effort may be of some consolation. It is then time to rejoice in your acceptances elsewhere and get ready to attend the college that has a seat with your name on it.

MAKING THE FINAL CHOICE

You've reached the point of making a final choice. As with most things in life, your choice is not completely irreversible in that you can always consider transferring to another college if the first choice isn't a good one. Remember, you won't be stuck at a particular college if you make a bad choice, but you should do your best to get it right the first time. Therefore, here are some tips to help you.

FIVE TIPS TO HELP YOU SELECT THE RIGHT COLLEGE

1. Visit or revisit the colleges. If you have yet to visit the colleges, this is an excellent time to take a close look. If you have visited the colleges whose offers you are considering, this may be an excellent time to revisit them. You may be amazed at how differently you view a college now that it wants you to join its community.

2. Talk to others, but listen to yourself. Gathering opinions from those you trust (family, graduates of the college, current students, your high school guidance counselor, teachers) is a good idea. Appreciate and respect the opinions of these

people, but remember that you are the one going to college. You need to make the best decision possible for yourself.

3. Read everything you can about the colleges. In fact, reread both the objective and subjective material discussed in Lesson 2. In doing so, you develop the balance between your reading perception and the opinions of others.

4. Review your college criteria. The criteria you selected months ago may well have changed after your initial college interview visits, in the course of applying and being accepted, and after your return trips to the colleges. Now is the time for you to reflect seriously on those, and other criteria, and their role in your decision-making process.

5. Don't forget to listen to yourself. After you've talked to everyone you wanted to talk to, reread viewbooks, and revisited the colleges, now is the time to stop and listen to your heart. When you do so, one college will emerge as your top choice. You have earned it—Go for it!

SUMMARY

In this lesson you learned the last four steps of the admission process: the last check before mailing your application, the seven things you can do while waiting that might increase your chances of admission, the types of responses to applications, and choosing your college.

Additional Admission Interviewer Questions Asked of You

1. How do you want to change in the next four years?

2. In what atmosphere do you learn best (with others or independently, with close attention from instructors or independently)?

3. What major problems exist in your high school today? What, if anything, can you do or are you doing about them?

4. What three characteristics of a college are most important to you and why?

5. Why did you select to become involved in particular activities?

6. If you could live the last four years of your life over again, what three changes would you make?

7. If you could meet with any decision maker in the world, who would you choose, why, and what would you hope to accomplish?

8. What have you learned about this college that you do not like?

9. Do you have any historical or contemporary heroes?

10. What two or three things would you change in society and why would you select these things?

ADDITIONAL QUESTIONS TO ASK OF THE ADMISSION INTERVIEWER

1. Does this college employ graduate students to teach undergraduates? Why or why not?

2. Which are your most popular academic departments?

3. Which are your most noteworthy departments (with national reputations)?

4. Does this college promote co-ed dorms? Why or why not?

5. What percentage of students live off campus, why, and what is the average cost?

6. What is the endowment of the college?

7. How has the endowment grown in the last five years?

8. What percentage of the freshmen graduate in four years? In five years?

9. Is the college pleased with these graduation rates? Why or why not?

10. What is the college doing to improve retention rates?

ADDITIONAL APPLICATION ESSAY OR PERSONAL STATEMENT QUESTIONS

1. Describe some special interest, experience, or achievement.

2. Describe a change you have noticed in your surroundings or in yourself.

3. Share with us the most difficult thing you have ever done.

4. What idea, concept, or theory has most influenced your life? Please share the influence.

5. Share with us your thoughts about your future and how they relate to your possible academic major.

6. What has been the most critical political or social movement in the last 250 years?

7. If you could create a holiday, what would you select, when would it be celebrated, and why would you make this selection?

8. If you could be anywhere in the world tomorrow, where would you choose and why?

9. If you could live at any point in history, when would you select and why?

10. Share with us the greatest challenge you have had to face.

SAMPLE OF A COMPLETED APPLICATION

Wonderful University

Application for Admission

Early Action (Due November 1)   Regular Decision (Due January 15)

Please circle one

Personal Information

Legal name: *O'Neal*   *Ashley*   *Joseph*   *M*   *Single*

               Last   *First*   *Middle*   *Sex*   *Marital Status*

Preferred to be called: *Ashley*   Social Security Number: *123-45-6789*

Date of Birth: *August 5, 1979*   Place of Birth: *State College, PA   USA*

                                               City   *State   Country*

Permanent Home Address: *1234 Your Street,*   *Big Deal   MO   56789*

                                 Street   *City*   *State*   *Zip*

Mailing (Boarding):   Box 155   1300 Academy Road   Culver IN   46511

                  Box   *Street*   *City*   *State Zip*

Permanent Home Phone: *(123) 456-7890*   Boarding Phone: *(987) 654-3210*

                     area code number   *area code number*

Applying for: Freshman Admission   Transfer Admission

                            (Please circle one)

Do you plan to apply for Financial Aid?   Yes   No

                                      circle one

                        If yes, forms filed on *1/15/96*

Citizenship: Country *USA*   If not a U.S. Citizen, what is your visa type?

The following is optional:

What is your first language if other than English?

Language spoken at home, if other than English?

Parents' country of birth: Mother: *USA*   Father: *USA*

Please circle how you would describe yourself:

African American or Black

American Indian or Alaskan Native

Asian or Pacific Islander

Hispanic or Latino

White, Anglo, or Caucasian

Other _____

Please specify

Parental Information

Name of Mother: *Debra Ann O'Neal*   Is she living?   *Yes*

Address (if different from your permanent address): *same*

Occupation: *Registered Nurse*   Employer: *Big City County Hospital*

Mother's College (if any): *Pierce College*   Degree: *AA* Year: *1970*

Graduate Studies: *Indiana University*   Degree: *RN* Year: *1972*

Name of Father: *Harry Frank O'Neal*   Is he living? *Yes*

Address (if different from your permanent address): *same*

Occupation: *High School Teacher*   Employer: *Big City High School*

Father's College (if any): *Wabash College*   Degree: *BA* Year: *1970*

Graduate Studies: *Indiana University*   Degree: *MA* Year: *1972*

With whom do you reside?: *my parents*

Sibling Information:

Name	Age	College	Year Graduate(d)
Frank O'Neal	*25*	*Dartmouth*	*1992*
Diane O'Neal	*23*	*UCLA*	*1994*
John O'Neal	*21*	*Notre Dame*	*1996*
Danielle O'Neal	*19*	*University of North Carolina–Chapel Hill*	*2000*
Jennifer O'Neal	*19*	*Stanford University*	*2000*

Educational Information

Name of school currently attending: *Culver Academy* Date Entered: *9/2/92*

Address of School: *1300 Academy Road, Culver, IN 46511*
Graduation Date: *6/4/96*

Name of Guidance Counselor: *Bradley Trevathan*

School Phone #: *(456) 789-1234*

List any additional colleges, high schools, or summer programs in which you have enrolled since 9th grade:

Name of Institution	Location (City, State, Zip)	Dates attended
None	—	—

Standardized Testing Information

It is important for us to receive your official standardized test scores. Please have these scores sent directly to us as soon as possible. Please indicate your standardized test history and future plans below:

SAT I *12/95 5/96 11/96*   SAT II *6/95 12/95*
ACT *12/95 4/96*   TOEFL *none*

Activities and Awards

Please use the area below to itemize your primary school, community, or employment activities in order of their interest to you.

Activity	Grade-level participation	Positions held	Continue in college?
School Newspaper	*12*	*Editor of Editorial Page*	*yes*
	11	*Advertisement Manager*	
	9, 10	*Writer*	
Student Council	*12*	*Class Vice President*	*yes*
	11	*School Treasurer*	
Varsity Baseball	*9, 10, 11*	*Pitcher*	*yes*
Church	*10, 11, 12*	*Lector at Monthly Service*	*possibly*
Community Service	*9, 10, 11, 12*	*Aide to Nurse's Aide*	*no*
McDonald's	*10, 11, 12*	*Counter Person*	*no*

Awards or Honors

- *National Honor Society—11*

- *Boy's State Representative—1 of 3 boys from county chosen to serve as representative at annual meeting—11*

- *All-County Pitcher (selected with record of 9 wins, 1 loss)—11*

- *Debbie Frole Prize for Community Service—12*

Part 2: Short Answer Questions

Please share with us your responses to the following questions:

1. How did you originally learn about Wonderful University?

    After long discussions with Mr. Trevathan, my high school guidance counselor, Wonderful University was strongly recommended to me based on size, location, setting, and my strong interest in business. My counselor said many students have attended Wonderful from my high school. He also said that many had my extracurricular interests in journalism, student government, and baseball. After carefully reviewing material from Wonderful, I became convinced that I needed to explore it further.

2. Briefly discuss your decision-making process and reasons for applying to Wonderful University.

    After reviewing a great deal of information from and about Wonderful, I added it to my list of colleges to visit. I did just that in the fall. While on campus I interviewed with Vicki Russell, Assistant Director of Admission. Her knowledge of Wonderful and sincere honesty impressed me a great deal. I was also very impressed when I visited a Mythology class taught by two professors, Kathy Lintner and Richard Davies. My parents and I also met with Cory Barnes, Associate Director of Financial Aid. He was very helpful in encouraging us to feel we could afford Wonderful. After considering all the colleges I visited, I decided to apply to Wonderful because of:

    - *the close relationship between the students and faculty*

    - *the modern and impressive facilities*

- *the excellent business program*

- *our sense that we could afford the college*

List other colleges to which you have applied or intend to apply. Also, in a word or two, share with us why you are interested in these colleges.

> *Wabash College—caring and involved faculty, wonderful tradition*
>
> *Depauw University—wonderful facilities, outstanding internships*
>
> *Marquette University—great city location, numerous opportunities*
>
> *Davidson University—excellent academic programs*
>
> *Colorado College—interesting one-course-at-a-time program.*

Please share with us those subjects you are most excited about exploring in college.

> *I have a great many academic interests in addition to business. My dad was a philosophy major in college, and we have had some exciting discussions in that area. In that I have always enjoyed writing and literature, I might also want to explore many courses in your English program.*

Briefly tell us about your experiences with a particular teacher, class, or project that has had special meaning for you.

> *Dr. Hodinko's class in Accounting Principles was especially fulfilling. Not only was Dr. Hodinko very demanding in terms of daily reading assignments and weekly tests, but we were expected to submit one major paper and host a 30-minute presentation of the paper to the class. It's interesting to learn just how far you can go when expectations are high. While it was a demanding class, I was also impressed at the time and availability Dr. Hodinko offered outside of class. I've been told that Dr. Hodinko's class is similar to a college course. If that is true, I feel better prepared having had this experience.*

We feel we can learn a great deal about a person by their favorite things. Recognizing that you might not have favorites in all of these areas, please include any other areas we might have missed:

book—*A River Runs Through It*

author—*Robert Ludlum*

film—*Field of Dreams*

athlete—*Cal Ripkin, Jr.*

team—*Pittsburgh Steelers and Colorado Rockies*

piece of music—*Emperor Concerto by Beethoven*

other—*time of day=morning (if rested and not rushed)*

other—*season=fall (crisp days with falling leaves)*

Please feel free to share any special circumstances the admission office should consider when reviewing your application.

When reviewing my academic record, you will notice a rather rocky start to my career at Culver. In addition to the adjustment of living away from home for the first time, I was also surprised by the very demanding nature of all my classes. I was fine after I learned how to manage my time, became less homesick, and made many new friends. I hope both my personal and academic development since my freshman year is a strong indication of my ability to do excellent work at Wonderful University.

Please share with us your career or professional plans.

As I mentioned earlier, I especially enjoyed Dr. Hodinko's course on Accounting Principles. This has led me to consider the possibility of specializing in this area of business. However, in that my knowledge of various other areas of business is very limited, I hesitate to make any plans at this point. I look forward to exploring the various areas and pursuing a career in business.

Part 3: The Essay or Personal Statement

If you could have lunch with any one person (living, dead, or fictional), who would it be and what would you discuss?

Throughout my life, I have been fascinated by Robert F. Kennedy. While I do not presume to note many similarities between his rich and eventful life and mine, common ground exists that leads me to believe this lunch would be informative and memorable.

During our lunch, I would like to focus upon three main issues:

- *his origin and compassion for the underrepresented*

- *his view of being overshadowed by older siblings*

- *his view of our present world*

In learning about Robert Kennedy, I have always been struck by his compassion for the underrepresented of not only this nation, but the world. From the text of his speeches in which he called for the abolishment of apartheid in South Africa in 1966, to his support for civil rights marchers in 1963, he seemed to be seeking justice for those who were victims of injustice. I am interested in learning where his passion for such issues developed. One might suggest that it is much easier for those blessed with wealth to be compassionate, but very few wealthy individuals made this their focal point as did he. Was there one defining moment or event in his life that shaped his view on this issue?

As one who is the youngest child with many talented siblings, I have felt overshadowed at times. With two older and talented brothers, did he ever feel overshadowed by them? In playing a major part in his brother's rise to the Presidency, and later as Attorney General, did he feel he was playing only a supporting role? I am also curious as to his motives for running for the Presidency. Did he feel that his brother's death left a void in the country that needed to be filled? Or rather, was he running because he felt a sincere desire to make his own contribution to the country?

Finally, I would ask his view of our world today. In what areas have we made progress that he would view as substantial? In what areas have we not only failed to make progress, but stepped backwards? As someone who played a significant role in the life of the nation in the 1960s, what words of counsel and advice can he offer someone who might choose to explore business or government service in the next century?

Robert Kennedy played an important role in American politics in the 1960s. Although he died nearly 30 years ago, he is viewed as a major example for many entering the world of politics today. I believe our meeting would be beneficial to me from a historical, political, and personal perspective.

Part 4: Secondary School Information

Form to be completed by your counselor requesting:

- relationship of counselor to you
- statement from counselor about your performance inside and outside the classroom
- view of your readiness to attend college

School Recommendation

Please share whatever you think is important for us to know about this applicant for admission to Wonderful University. Please focus upon personal qualities and academic ability. Any insight in assisting us in differentiating this student from others in the graduating class is especially appreciated.

From the first day I met Ashley, I knew he had the ability of making a very positive impact on our school, while obtaining a first-rate education. I was right. He has done an excellent job in the classroom while playing a major role in many extracurricular activities.

As a student—*Ashley has earned a B+ average (3.45) while taking accelerated courses in both English and biology. One of the few members of the junior class to earn National Honor Society recognition, it is easy to understand why Dr. Bernie Hodinko shared these words about Ashley's performance in his Accounting Principles class:*

Ashley is the kind of young person who knows what it takes to be successful. His hard work and daily diligence in this demanding class led to one of the highest grades earned this year. I am especially proud of Ashley's willingness to offer his time and talents to those students who struggled with the material. Here is a very bright young man who truly cares for others.

In addition to his strong grades, Ashley has performed well in both standardized tests. His 1200 on the SAT and 28 on the ACT simply reconfirm his strong intellectual ability.

Outside the classroom—*What can you say about a student leader, with a penchant for journalism, who is blessed with a golden pitching arm? Ashley's leadership abilities have grown since his involvement in Student Government began last year. Elected to two offices in two years, many look to him for leadership and guidance. Ashley has been a member of our school newspaper staff since freshman year. His most recent position is that of Editor of the Editorial Page. This is an excellent match for him because he never hesitates to encourage an honest exchange of opinions, particularly those of the underrepresented. His record of 9 wins in 10 decisions last spring led our team to the league championship and All-County honors for Ashley.*

A member of a very talented family that stresses education, Ashley is the youngest of 6 children who have attended colleges such as Stanford, Notre Dame, UCLA, the University of North Carolina, and Dartmouth. His family supports Ashley in his efforts to gain admission to selective colleges. Simply put, he has set high academic aspirations for himself. While undecided in his career goals, he tends to lean toward business.

Ashley O'Neal is a very special young man both inside and outside the classroom. Please give him careful consideration. He will be a welcome addition to your community as he has been to ours. He has my highest recommendation.

Teacher Evaluation of Applicant

To the student: After completing name, addresses, and waiver, please give this form to a teacher who has taught you English, languages, mathematics, science, history, or social studies in the last two years.

Applicant's Name: *O'Neal   Ashley   Joseph*
                          Last   First   Middle

Applicant's Permanent Address: *1234 Your Street   Big City   MO   56789*
                                   Street   City   State Zip

Name and Address of High School:
         Culver Academy   1300 Academy Rd.   Culver   IN   45611
          School   Street   City   State   Zip

I waive   I do not waive (circle one) my right of access to this report under the Family Rights and Privacy Act of 1974

_____

Signature of Applicant   *Date*

How long have you known the applicant? *I have known the applicant for 2 years*

In what course(s) have you taught the applicant? *American Government*

What two words come to mind when describing the applicant? *diligent and caring*

Counselor's Name: *Ralph Manuel*   Title: *Social Studies Teacher*

Signature: _____ Department Telephone: *(789) 765-4321*

Please share with us your view of this applicant as a student in your classroom. We are especially interested in your opinion of the student's:

- intellectual strengths and weaknesses
- ability to convey ideas in writing
- strengths in relation to others in the class
- ability to handle college-level work at this institution

Ashley O'Neal was a member of my American Government class during his junior year at Culver. Over the course of the year his strengths, both intellectual and personal, became more evident, whereas his weaknesses seemed to diminish.

Among his many strengths, perhaps the most notable were his:

- *determination to arrive in class totally prepared each day*
- *ability to analyze complex concepts*
- *talent for clear, detailed writing*
- *genuine concern for assisting others in understanding the material*

When considering areas of weakness, I would say that Ashley needed to focus upon:

- *ability to memorize names and dates*
- *more patience with others holding different ideas than his*

While his strengths are impressive, I most admire Ashley's ability and interest in addressing the two areas of weakness. When these were pointed out to him during an evaluation meeting in the fall, he worked hard to improve both his memory and patience. As a result, he became an even stronger student.

I was especially proud of two particular situations. Ashley worked diligently to create perhaps the finest term paper I have received in years. His 26-page paper analyzing the writings of Robert F. Kennedy was simply remarkable. He enjoyed working on the paper so much, he went above and beyond the project requirement and created a fifteen-minute video presentation on the life of Mr. Kennedy. Simply put, a spark was lit and it grew into a flame.

The second situation dealt with Ashley's creation of a study group for the less-interested students. He quietly formed this group, held weekly sessions, and assisted the students in preparing for examinations. To this day, he is unaware of both my knowledge of the group, or the high regard these students have for him. He simply took it upon himself to assist others.

Ashley O'Neal is ready to attend college. He has done an excellent job here. He will be missed by many of us. I give him my highest recommendation.

Rating of Student

Please rate the student in relation to his or her performance in your class:

Characteristic	Below Average	Good	Very Good	Excellent	Rare
Creative, Original Thought		x			
Intellectual Ability				x	
Written Expression				x	
Disciplined Work Habits			x		
Sense of Humor		x			
Enthusiasm in School Work				x	
Breadth of Knowledge			x		
Inquiring Attitude			x		
Working with Others				x	
Problem-Solving Ability			x		
Energy			x		

EVALUATION SUMMARY

If you would like to share anything else with a member of the Admission Office Staff at Wonderful University, please ____ here, or call us at (800) won-derU.

Thank you for taking the time to complete this teacher evaluation.

Rating of Student

Please rate the student in relation to his or her entire graduating class:

Characteristic	Below Average	Good	Very Good	Excellent	Rare
Academic Achievement				x	
Motivation					x
Emotional Maturity			x		
Leadership				x	
Initiative					x
Sense of Humor			x		
Concern for Others				x	
Reaction to Criticism				x	

Please attach a current high school transcript with

- all high school courses and grades
- designation of accelerated courses
- all standardized test results

Peer Reference

Name of Applicant: *Ashley O'Neal*   Social Security Number: *123-45-6789*

High School: *Culver Academy*   *Culver*   *IN*   *45611*
                  Name   City   State   Zip

Peer: Thank you for completing this recommendation. We view this form as a vehicle through which we can become better acquainted with members of our applicant pool. In that we take your words seriously, please choose them carefully. This reference will not be shared with anyone other than members of the admission office at Wonderful University.

Name of Peer: *John Friley*   Signature of Peer: _____

How long have you known the applicant?
I have known Ashley for four years.

In what context have you known the applicant?
As a friend, classmate, and teammate.

What are the first words or phrases that come to mind in describing the applicant?
Ashley is intelligent, fun, hard working, and cares a lot about others.

Please provide an example of a particular strength and weakness of the student.
Strength—Ashley has the ability to perform well in class, write a good editorial, pitch a great baseball game, and spend quality time with his many friends—all in the same day! He can balance so many things well.

Weakness—Ashley forgets to make time for himself. He is always so very busy that many of his friends really worry about him. He rarely misses a day of school or work at McDonald's, but maybe the rest would serve him well.

What else would you like us to know about the applicant?
He is well liked and respected by a wide variety of students.

Parent(s) Recommendation

Name of Applicant: *Ashley O'Neal*   Social Security Number: *123-45-6789*

High School: *Culver Academy   Culver   IN   45611*
                    Name   City   State   Zip

Parent(s): Thank you for completing this recommendation. We view this form as a vehicle through which we can become better acquainted with members of our applicant pool. In that we take your words seriously, please choose them carefully. Please feel welcome to complete this recommendation either individually or together. This reference will not be shared with anyone other than members of the admission office at Wonderful University.

Name of Parent(s): *Debra O'Neal and Harry O'Neal*   Date: _____

Signature(s) of Parent(s):   _____

Please share with us the first words that come to mind describing your son or daughter.

Caring Active Bright Ambitious

Please share with us whatever you want us to know about your son or daughter.

Ashley is the youngest of six children. All of our other children have excelled inside and outside the classroom. While he is no exception, Ashley has developed a greater sense of balance by pursuing student government, athletics, and journalism. We are proud of this balance and view it as somewhat unique among our children.

Ashley cares deeply for others. This is especially true of those people in need. Without urging from us, he obtained a 20-hour-per-week job at McDonald's. When we asked him why, he said that he wanted to learn life from all perspectives. Little did we know that he donates half of his pay to the local homeless shelter. We were told this by the person who runs the shelter. To this day, Ashley does not know that we have learned this about him.

We are very proud of our son. While we both agree that he extends himself a bit too far, we are amazed at all he accomplishes. At times, we just shake our heads in wonder.

We hope our comments have allowed you to get to know this special person a bit better. Thank you for the opportunity to share our views of him.

Character Recommendation

Name of Applicant: *Ashley O'Neal*   Social Security Number: *123-45-6789*

High School: *Culver Academy*   *Culver*   *IN*   *45611*
                         Name   City   State   Zip

Please give this form to an adult who knows you well. Many applicants use this form to solicit a recommendation from neighbors, coaches, ministers, rabbis, friends of the family, etc. The only guidance we offer is that we hope to gain a different perspective of the applicant from someone other than peers, parents, teachers, or counselors.

Dear Adult:

Thank you for completing this recommendation. We view this form as a vehicle through which we can become better acquainted with members of our applicant pool. In that we take your words seriously, please choose them carefully. This reference will not be shared with anyone other than members of the admission office at Wonderful University.

Name of Adult: *John Babcock*

Signature: Date

How long have you known the applicant?
   I have known Ashley for eight years.

In what context have you known the applicant?
   Ashley O'Neal has been my neighbor and employee for eight years. I remember the first time I met Ashley. Within one week from moving into the neighborhood, he came to the door and asked if he could mow my lawn. I'll never forget wondering how that skinny, small kid would manage to mow my large lot. Well, I gave him the opportunity and have never regretted my decision. He is as reliable as a clock.

As the owner and manager of the local McDonald's, he came to ask me about another job two years ago. I knew he was active in lots of things at school, but with his track record on my lawn, I gave him a shot. Well, my faith was again well placed. Ashley works 20 hours per week and hasn't missed a day in two years. I have always been impressed with the way he works with others. His patience, kindness, and genuine concern about them is refreshing.

Ashley O'Neal is one great person. I don't know much about your university, but I do know that he will make you proud.

INDEX